AF256267

"Leadernomics" - Leadership For Human Beings

By Nick Hewyn Holmes

Leadernomics and Scrumnastics:

"Harnessing the unique power of the team to unearth and unleash as yet undreamt-of wealth, technology, products and services for the benefit of all."

ISBN-13: 978-1-9161604-2-2

Published by Scrumnastics Press
792, Wilmslow Road, Didsbury.
Manchester. M20 6UG
United Kingdom.

For Carol, Sam, Matthew and Sian. Thanks for putting up with your dad while he made yet another completely bonkers book project come to life

My grandfather, Jack Bowen, who was a 'Clerk of Works.' He oversaw the building of Cwmbran New Town in the 1950's and 1960's. He divided all people into just two types: Talkers and Do-ers.

Every night he would bring huge, blue inked, incredibly complicated drawings home with plans for shopping centres, roads, roundabouts, schools, freshwater pipelines, foul water pipelines, gas mains and electricity pylon lines for the new town of Cwmbran.

When I asked him what they were for he would say, "Nick, I have to make these high-fallutin' plans for the pen-pushers, who don't know what they are doing, so that they keep out of the hair of the skilled builders, who actually DO know what they are doing."

That taught me, as a five-year-old, almost everything I ever needed to learn about talkers and do-ers and how you need to treat them differently.

This book is for the do-ers, I hope it helps you do even **_more_**.

"When bad men combine, the good must associate; else they will fall one by one, an unpitied sacrifice in a contemptible struggle." - Edmund Burke.

And also, Mr Marsh, of Clytha Infants and Junior school, who taught us seven year olds about leadership and taking responsiblity. He also spoke to us (although we didn't understand a word of it at the time) about peacetime and wartime officers. I may not have understood any of it then, but, being seven and impressionable, nevertheless it stayed with me until I could understand all of what he taught us.

He was a wise man.

CONTENTS

Contents

Foreword

I have worked with Nick Holmes in several large-scale (to be honest, humongous scale) operations. Usually with the kind of pressure heaped upon him that no-one really deserves or wants.

The way out of a pressure cooker environment is through management, when the pressure is on, the stars shine and correct methods come to the surface, it really is that simple. And handling such pressure using Nick's application method of using Scrum is key to productivity.

No method is fool proof, it is how you apply the system that counts and can you apply and improve productivity instead of just applying a methodology for its own sake.

Nick's use of Scrum and Agile techniques is unique, using the methodology to manage people, tasks, events and the often-encountered surprises of an everyday work cycle and smoothing over and managing the crises before they are even acknowledged as such. What a lot of managers always miss out is the handling of people, well without handling people correctly the rest of it all falls apart.

Agile process are often looked at as widget production techniques, used for "the guys in the back" who are producing something tangible, but people are and always will be the focus of any management methodology, but people just don't know it. Nick does, and his book highlights it.

Nick's book differs from most other Scrum books out there, because it is not just teaching you the processes (called events, formerly ceremonies) and the roles, but showing you how they should be used, who should be involved and why involving the correct people and attributing them to the correct roles produces results, and more importantly how involving the incorrect people does not.

Nick approaches the problems of scrum in a humorous, but accurate and factual way. Ensuring that productivity is the focus of the teaching. Whether your teams are close at hand, or remote, management is the key to ensuring that they are productive at all times. Scrum can achieve this, but scrum used in Nick's manner ensures this.

There is nothing worse than a dry lecture or a dry book or a dry tutorial, Nick's book is the exact opposite – it's meant to be enjoyed and absorbed, there are great stories, all relevant, showing the correct approach to adopting Scrum and making it work, for you, at the optimum.

Read the book, enjoy it, but more than anything else – Apply what you've learned.

Laurie Williams M.Sc., Senior Programme Manager, Agile Alliance Certified Scrum Master, Knowledge Management advocate.

Acknowledgements

A huge amount of thanks go to a lot of people who encouraged me to write this book. Chief among them are:

Carol Ann Holmes for simply years of support. You are a star. Thank you with all my heart.

Sam, Matthew, and Sian for putting up with your dad while writing this. Actually, now I come to think of it, thanks for putting up with dad full stop. And Ursula Thomas ('Auntie Urf"), the Mary Poppins of Upper Cwmbran, for never not believing in me.

Father Nicholas Pearkes, Bob Seaman, Sacha and Graeme, all in south Devon. Many thanks too.

And to Peter Littlechild, raconteur, Pelforth beer connoisseur, fount of knowledge of all things Welsh, and finest beer mate that anyone at Wissant's Chez Nichole could ever have. Cheers bwtti!

A special thank you to the hundreds of people I have trained, coached and mentored over the years. Your input made every one of the courses, and all of this book so much better than it would have otherwise been.

And finally, whatever mistakes there are in here in this book, they are mine and mine alone.

"Nick joined a de-motivated team with unclear processes... within 2-3 weeks he had made a huge impact on morale and within 6 weeks had doubled output per person."

Nick Hewyn Holmes

Nick Hewyn Holmes is an ex-programmer and Data Miner (he was personally trained by Ralph Kimball and is a graduate of Kimball university).

He has been doing Agile Project Management since 1995 when he was working for Panasonic Europe. He has been building and running completely remote Agile Scrum teams since 2016 for Global 500, Government and small companies.

How that started was that Nick was the European Middle East and Africa (EMEA) project manager for the first rollout of remote offices for a global petrochemical company in 1996.

Nick was the Europe, Middle East and Africa (EMEA) Project Manager for the EMEA part of the world-wide, and first rollout of remote working sales office service for a Global company. For that role his territory was every office in every major city between Dublin and Moscow and from Stockholm down to Cairo.

He was lead project manager for the UK Government's Department for Education "Get Help With Tech" project during the lockdowns. He and his multi entity team of private, public, and government partners was tasked to deliver 500,000 Apple iPads, Chromebooks, and laptops to the poorest school children in England within 6 months in order to try and mitigate the effects of lockdown. They delivered 550,000 - and within four months.

While doing projects for IBM at the DVLA he was programme manager for the £15 million removal of the 40+ million paper driving licences, and also MOT 2 (30+ million vehicles examined and annually recorded).

He has even used Scrum to lead, manage and run rock bands. It is easier to herd cats than to lead and manage musicians. If he can do this for rock stars, then you can probably guess he knows how to get you to do the same for your rock stars.

Nick has been doing Japanese style management since 1995, where he learned it while consulting for a data sciences company for a project at Panasonic Europe. He's been doing Agile, Lean and Scrum from that time, and he has been running teams that work remotely on a full-time basis since 2016.

He was an Information Technology Manager at 29, Information Technology Director at 32, and a Managing Director at 35. He has been a running various companies as a managing director ever since (30+ years).

He has worked offering management consultancy for the Bank Of England, Barclaycard, HSBC, Ministry of Defence, Driver and Vehicle Licencing Agency, Department for Education, Dow Chemical, IBM,

Cognos, Astra Pharmaceuticals, Boehringer-Ingelheim, ICI, Christian Salvesen, Royal National Pension Fund For Nurses, Zurich Re, Co-operative Insurance Services, Thomas Cook Travel and Panasonic Europe, amongst others.

These days he runs his own leadership group, teams, and trains, coaches and mentors online Agile teams for clients under the "Scrumnastics" banner. He writes his books for those that can't afford him in the hope that ,if people do what he says in the book then, one day they **will** be able to afford him.

He has a absurd passion for both steel and aluminium-bodied Jaguar V8s , Honda engines, Toyota production management and tries his very best not to die horribly whilst sailing the cold, cold, and treacherous coast of the United Kingdom.

Before Rock and Roll died, he was also guitarist, singer and songwriter for the finest male-menopause rock band in the world, the Nick Holmes Band.

He is the author of three books, which are:

"Scrumnastics - Successfully Lead And Manage Remote, In-Office, & Hybrid Teams Using Scrum"

"Going Agile - Going Agile Without Breaking The Bank Or Breaking Your Heart"

"Leadernomics - Leadership For Human Beings" (this one).

How to Contact:

Substack: substack.com/@nickhewynholmes
   X (Twitter) @HewynNick
   Websites www.nickhewynholmes.com
   www.scrumnastics.com

Testimonials For Nick Hewyn Holmes

1: "The best manager I have ever had." **C Shepherd, Barclays Secured Loan.**

2: "Nick joined a de-motivated team with unclear processes... within 2-3 weeks he had made a huge impact on morale and within 6 weeks had doubled output per person. More importantly, his management legacy means that the high standards continued after he left" - **Infrastructure Portfolio Manager (Grade 6) DVLA.**

3: "Nick has an amazing knack of managing complexity. Drawing on keen analytical and technical skills and first-rate people skills, he has been able to guide us through a Discovery and give us confidence that our direction, although unexpected, was not just legitimate but ground-breaking. He has also generously coached key team members, leaving behind an agile legacy and an enthusiastic team!" **Assistant Director, Pupil Premium Strategy, Department for Education.**

4: "Nick was a great asset to our modernisation work in Department for Education. He initially focussed on leading a ministerial initiative through Discovery phase and early Alpha phase work.

During that time, he pushed hard for user need and developed a route forward which would allow low risk development that allowed Department for Education the best of both worlds; to aim for an end-state solution but build in a number of phases that meant we could look at how industry evolved to our plans.

Following his impact on that area, we retained Nick to help us progress thinking on moving from 'projects in silos' to blending resource and governance across services more readily.

My staff found Nick insightful and knowledgeable, as well as a great coach. He helped me identify leadership challenges and opportunities as a second pair of eyes."   - **Deputy Director, Data**

Modernisation Division, Data Group, Department for Education.

5: "You can give Nick Holmes any business problem and he will always come up with a solution." **Pete Lumley - Thomas Cook Travel**

6: "I can vouch that, as a manager, you're definitely not a psychopath. Some people I've worked with think good management is finding a spark of a problem, let it take hold or even fan the flames and then get everyone to drop everything to man the hoses to put out the fire and then tell everyone how good they are at fixing problems. Not you. You sort it quietly." **N. Griffiths, - Analytics Team, FirstPlus Financial.**

Leadership

"Men in cloth caps and overalls built this country; men in suits with briefcases destroyed it." - Fred Dibnah (allegedly)

Or, to put it another way, you really don't have to wear a suit to be a leader (and the very best ones never have).

Introduction

Private Cole: "Why is it us? Why Us?"

Colour Sergeant Bourne: "Because we're here, lad. Nobody else. Just us."
(- "Zulu," 1964).

Welcome. Stepping up to take on any leadership is a bit like the above quotation from the 1964 film, "Zulu."

Why are you here? Why is it us? Why us?

"Because we're here, lad. Nobody else. Just us."

So…

You're about to face a group of people for the very first time whom you are going to lead and manage. There's no-one else to do it.

Your heart is beating in your chest, your stomach is jumping up and down. Your throat is dry, you feel slightly sick and you're also probably younger than many of them.

* * *

Eek!

You've got that classic fight or flight response and, inside, you don't know whether to stay or run away.

Double Eek.

But,… this time it's going to be alright. Why?

Because you have put the work in to read this book, which means that you know what you will need to do in order to get them to allow you to lead them. Which is unlike the story of the last bloke.

You know that, unlike them, you won't need to use things like a silly posh voice, you won't need to pathetically try and overpower and dominate your team with your "strong" personality, you won't have to make them feel small. Best of all, you will never need to behave like a psychopath, ever.

Unlike the last leader, you know that the key to being a successful leader is largely down to practicing a craft, just like, say, carpentry, or plastering, or bricklaying. In other words, it is a combination of various practical things: you need some specialist knowledge, some practical skills, the right attitude, and, most of all, you need to practice, practice, and practice. My view is that it is a job which has more in common with being a mechanic, an electrician, a builder or a computer programmer than trying to be Ming the Merciless, ruler of the universe.

Let's get one thing clear: it has been my experience that there are a great deal more people in our society who _can_ lead than actually _do_ lead. Leadership is not for everyone and not everyone can do it. However, there are many who can lead but don't want to. That has more to do with desire for it, and where they are in life right now than ability. For example, parents have to lead heir children every day - and there are a lot of them.

Oh, and one more thing, you need ___Trust. - And most people do not trust their leaders.___

* * *

You are going to have to work very hard to get them to trust you. The kind of trust where they know that they can *rely* on you, that you will do your best for them, that you won't betray them and that you are working to bring out the best in them and for them and not doing it for yourself.

Like I said,, you are going to have to work very hard.

Oh, and you are going to do that in a work environment, where your team's every good instinct is not to trust you. Why not? Because at least one of them will already have been betrayed by an unreliable, or downright dishonest former leader/manager.

Note to self: if you have been betrayed in your work life this will make you a MUCH better leader than you would otherwise be.

But, because of all the knowledge you you will have, you will be able to balance the fear you feel inside against the sure faith that you will be able to convince your new team that you know how to guide them, protect them, do the very best for them and put them and their interests before your own.

Do that and you will have cracked it. You _will_ be a great leader.

And that is what this book is all about.

It's probably very hard for you to believe but when I was a kid, leadership started early - almost all kids everywhere were taught leadership - both in their schools and also in their wider social groups like the Wolf Cubs, Scouts and even church, if they went.

That's another thing that was different: there were loads and loads of leaders and leadership was practiced at every level. It was expected of you.

This wasn't just done in posh schools such as Eton and Harrow, but it was done in everyday, middling, normal state schools like the one I went to.

* * *

It was expected of small boys and girls that you would know and learn a bit about leadership - just as much as it was also expected that you were going to learn to read, learn to spell or learn your times tables. This state of affairs was entirely normal for all children of my, and previous generations.

You have to bear in mind that children were viewed differently back then. (By the way, it was not particularly comfortable thing.) Children were viewed as being completely useless and so irrelevant until they proved themselves useful, so if you were a kid then you knew you had better become useful - and quickly. So we did.

So seven year olds all over the country began to learn the basics of how to lead other seven year olds and so start to become leaders.

So what? Well, the point is, if you can teach the basics of good leadership to seven year olds how hard can leadership be for adults to learn? It can't be too hard, can it?

Key point: Leadership is not for academics - leadership is for people who need to get things done that are too large to get done by themselves - this is for practical people who have practical things to achieve in a practical manner.

Unfortunately, gradually, over decades, this simple idea of teaching and instilling leadership into normal, every day kids has evaporated from school timetables and social organisations.

This book is meant to help you bring back leadership - not just for yourself - but for everyone around you too. We don't need a few wonderful leaders - we need hundreds of thousands, perhaps millions of them. This is a book for real, normal human beings who either want (or have been chosen) to take on a leadership role whether they like it or not - and want to make a great job of it.

The likelihood is that you will be working in some kind of small-ish team, so it will be unlikely that your organisation can afford to have you as a full time leader. You will probably still be doing your original job alongside being a leader.

* * *

But that's fine. Unlike what most management 'gurus' say, about leaders not actually 'doing' anything, you will still be able to do both. In fact, until you are leading larger groups which can generate enough profit that it can afford the luxury of having you do it full time, leadership is not really a full time job - simply because your company or organisation won't be able to afford you to be a full time leader until then.

For you, much of doing a job of leadership boils down to:

1. Giving the people in your charge a vision of where you are all going

2. Giving clear, day-to-day directions and instructions on how to get there

3. Increasing their sense of status by doing things like giving an encouraging nod of the head, the odd understanding smile and making sure that they know that you are defending them at every turn.

If, at a later stage, your organisation becomes profitable enough to allow you to be a full time leader then the things you will learn here will still be applicable. Very applicable. People who can lead small teams can lead huge groups - but please take note, it doesn't always go the other way around.

Why do we need lots of new, great leaders right now? Well, look around you. - Exactly. Enough said.

Please don't worry if you're you're the kind of person who would rather do their original "proper job," where you can do some "proper work," rather than any of this airey-fairey, not-getting-your-hands-dirty leadership stuff.

We call this type of person in my company a 'reluctant leader.' Good for you, you are exactly the sort of person this book is for and you are going to be great.

How do I know? Because the vast majority of the people I have trained over the years are exactly like you. Most real leaders with true capability are the same. Remember, in the army, corporals and sergeants don't start off as corporals and sergeants, they start off as soldiers.

Oh, one thing I have to tell you: if you are a 'do-er,' unfortunately, you will never get the same level of satisfaction of a job well done as you would if you did it yourself. Every bit of satisfaction that you get from your team's achievements will come to you second hand. Sorry, it just does but you will get used to that.

By the way, even by the end of this introduction section, you will also know more about how to be a great leader than 80% of existing British leaders.

How can I say that? Because I and my colleagues have to train all sorts of leaders and frankly, when it comes to great leadership people like you don't exactly have a great deal of competition. And we know that because we have all had to work for 'that boss,' haven't we?

It's sad to say that the present crop of British business and political leaders are probably some of the worst in the world - it wasn't always like that - but it is today.

Unfortunately, Even Leaders Have To Talk About Economics Sometimes

Let's be clear: bad leadership costs us, all of us, a fortune every year. A fortune this country can not afford to squander anymore. It costs us in all sorts of ways such as bad productivity, bad morale, delays, confusion, the creation and delivery of sub-standard work, missed delivery times, and awful quality in both products and services.

It is pretty obvious that here in Britain and in Europe we are in an economic malaise. So how do we get out of it?

Crudely, there are only two ways. To change things for the better we can either cut everything that government spends money on, or are going to have to make our economy grow. Which would you rather do?

Growth has to be the only way forward, doesn't it? So we need to grow our economy through our people, growing our small and medium sized companies and, as a net result of that, our country's economy.

The really great thing in our favour is that we have some of the best workers that this country has ever had. These people also have the finest productivity multiplying and labour saving tools, materials, and techniques that have ever existed. This means they have the ability to be more productive than any British, American, Australian, or New Zealand worker from past generations.

For example, my father was an engineer and an oil driller, my uncles were electricians, fitters, mechanics plumbers, bricklayers and every trade. They would have given their eye-teeth for access to the incredible, affordable tools and modern techniques and materials that modern workers have access to.

So with people like that, we can be assured that we have all the potential to grow that we need.

The key, core problem we all face is the product of bad leadership and management. It costs us a fortune. And while we are squandering that fortune we are not growing - we are diminishing.

The easiest and cheapest way to achieve growth and productivity is to motivate our people to increase their productivity by getting rid of lousy leadership and management and replacing it with great leadership and management so that the people who actually do the real, productive work that makes a difference and makes the money can do that in the best and most efficient way possible.

And Back To Leadership Again - (Phew)

But here's a warning for all of us: Part of the reason that there are so many bad leaders (and managers) is because too many of the normal people (like you and I) have not put ourselves forward to lead - yet.

* * *

Why is that? Well, from talking to many of our students I can tell you that many of us think leadership and management as all rather "icky." We would rather do our 'proper jobs.' It is also seen as rather boring and dull, and it attracts the boring and dull too.

It is also the case that most of the people who should be leaders think that leadership and managment are boring. Worse, because of that thought it attracts really boring people, and that is a real problem.

I also think part of the problem is that what is understood to be leadership and management actually isn't that - it is administration and bureaucracy - no wonder it attracts the boring.

But I am afraid those days are over - we really can't afford to carry on like this. If we don't swim then we are going to sink.

I am here to tell you that great leaders and managers should be dynamic and full of energy, and you should stop following every rule, crossing every "t", and dotting every "i."

Here we go.

Cut to the chase, Nick

I promised you that I would give you more knowledge here than 80% of existing leaders, so here we go:

Crucial First Point:

"You manage things; you lead people." - Grace Brewster Murray Hopper[1]

Got that? If you remember nothing more from this book than the

---

[1] Co-inventor of the COBOL programming language and a Commodore in the US Navy - so she would know.

sentence above then you will turn out to be a better natural leader than 80% of the 'leaders' that I have ever come across.

Why?

Because so many leaders try to do their job by doing it the other way around - they manage people rather than leading them. - And that never works. Why? Because leadership is about dealing properly with people, not treating them as 'resources' like machines. (And project managers, I am especially talking to you here).

Leadership is not hard once you know how to do it, it is just that most people, especially in business, don't know how to do it because they have never been taught how to properly. - Not any more.

Remember: Manage things, lead your people.

It's working people that create the things that create wealth, not the company's annual staff review.

Geving your people a dream of where you are going is and example of leadership. Getting them to fill in a staff survey is management.

Crucial Second Point:

My job is to give you the quickest route to being a great leader, so let me use an idea that I use in the first ten minutes on my leadership course for new leaders.

Here it is: Don't think about your job as being a leader as such, think about you job as being the captain of a sports team.

What is the prime reason to be in a team? To win. Who inspires the team to win? The captain.

What are some of the things that a captain of a sports team has to do?

* * *

Amongst other things they must:

Inject enthusiasm into them, at all times, especially on that soggy wet Wednesday in February
Encourage them, (literally "give heart,") especially when they are not winning
Inspire them to go on and achieve greater and greater success
Develop a team spirit, or camaraderie
Convince them that you are doing this for them, not for you
Have a quiet word with the underperformers, when necessary

If you think of the job in terms like being a captain of a sports team then leading becomes a lot easier, doesn't it?

And finally…

As the great Clive James, one of my favourite authors once said, "you don't have to be po-faced in order to be serious."

In my work I can occasionally be a very irreverent person, as you will shortly see. But please don't think that when I am being irreverent I am not being incredibly serious about what I am saying.

Leadership and management are dry subjects, and sometimes can be boring. (No, really, they can…). My job is to give you as much knowledge as I can as quickly as I can.

So I will sometimes use humour and irreverence to get across some otherwise very dry and boring points.

I believe that great leadership and management are not only going to be the key to getting us, all of us, out of the economic malaise we find ourselves in but the cheapest investments and biggest bangs for the buck you can possibly make to make that change.

Always remember that, just like it says on the cover, my goal is not to make you another Winston Churchill, but to avoid you becoming another little Hitler.

So I wish you a fab and groovy start to your new career.

By the way, this craft of leadership has to be practiced and honed over time. If you practice you will be a much better leader in twenty years time than you will be tomorrow. Remember how long after you passed your driving test it took you to actually learn to drive? It is the same here.

Before we start properly, may I leave you with two quotes from one of Britain's greatest leaders, Winston Churchill.

"Success consists of going from failure to failure without loss of enthusiasm."

And

"Success is not final, failure is not fatal, it is the courage to continue that counts."

- Winston Churchill

Wise words

Cheers!

Nick - January 2025

LET'S START AT THE VERY BEGINNING - (IT'S A VERY
GOOD PLACE TO START...)

Leadership and "Leadernomics"

"Management is doing things right; leadership is doing the right thing."
—*Peter F. Drucker - twentieth century management guru*

First, an aside:

Why Is This Book Called "Leadernomics," And Where Does The Weird Word "Leadernomics" Come From?

In case you were wondering, "**Leadernomics**" is the name of our leadership training course that we give to our clients when we manage one or more of their projects. We put everyone through it, including our staff.

The word "Leadernomics" is something I made up from combining the two words, "Nomics," and "Leader":

Nomics means "deep knowledge of," or "relating to the laws of," or "Having the general force of natural law" (originally from the Greek word "**nomos**").

Leader - means to do with leadership and leaders.

The intended outcome is that if you as a leader follow these laws then you will be able to successfully and competently lead a team, any team, and lead them well and convincingly.

Why Do *You* Need To Know About Leadership?

In a word, much greater productivity for your team. Where does that increase in productivity come from? Greater capability and greater capacity to do things. What makes these two appear? Great leadership first, and then great management second.

* * *

It is not rocket science. People work better if they have clear instructions, clear rules and clear direction than if they have unclear instructions, unclear rules and unclear direction.

Why do we need these things now? Well, look around us - we are in an economic mess, and personally, I think things are going to get worse before they can get better. Perhaps a great deal worse.

But the thing is, we really shouldn't be in this mess. Today we have the most skilled and talented "do-ers," (such as tradespeople and IT people,) and they have the most incredible sets of tools (which they know how to use) at their disposal. This (and a squillion videos on YouTube) makes them far more productive than the engineers and tradespeople of my father's, uncles', and grandfathers' generations ever were.

Yet here we are. But why?

Two reasons:

1.   Unfortunately, unlike, say, the Japanese, (who take leadership and management VERY seriously, as they regard it as their very special secret sauce,) the techniques of leadership and management as practiced in Britain are a mess and always have been. Worse, even in the twenty-first century, we still see echoes of the old British class system. Unfortunately, at the very core of the class system, to be a do-er is to have a _much_ lower status than a talker.

2.   Because of this in Britain, as I have said many times elsewhere, leadership (and management) often attract _exactly_ the wrong kind of people: precisely those who are actually the least suited to it. I expect you know them well, these are the boring, self-serving, status-hungry, rule-following jobsworths.

How do I know? My colleagues and I are leadership, management and project management consultants. We fix failing projects in the private and government sectors and it is our job to make them succeed. That is our job, and we have worked from Orlando to Moscow and from Stockholm to Cairo - and all points in between.

* * *

Sometimes we are called in at the beginning of an endeavour, and are often called on to create brand-new project teams, complete with new project leads, new managers and new workers too. We also rescue projects that have gone wrong. What is the main reason for a project going wrong? It is not the workers, it's the bad or incompetent leadership and management.

Unfortunately, British leadership and management is largely awful because British companies won't train their leaders and managers, and if they do, they train them at universities.

But leadership and management are not academic subjects - they are practical, human facing skills - ask the Japanese who are acknowledged to be the best in the world at leadership and management. And that is the reason why we are where we are - so we need new people, lots and lots of new people, to be leaders and managers and we need a different and better quality of person to be leaders and managers. In other words, YOU.

This can be done - and it can be done here in Britain. I and my staff have taken over teams and DOUBLED the amount of work they get through inside six weeks. When we do it we don't require any other investment other than our time.

How have we achieved this? Is it because we are brilliant leaders and managers? Well, this is what we do for a job but here's a secret: you don't actually have to be brilliant - you just have to be better than your competitors at leadership - and they are almost all terrible at it. So to become a better leader than almost everybody else you just have to not be terrible. - And that's not too high a bar to get over, is it?

To illustrate, in our classes we tell the old story of two guys in the woods running from a bear. The guy who lives isn't the one who can outrun the bear - the one who survives is the one who can outrun the other guy.

So, we offer you two proven methods of increasing productivity in book form which really work and don't cost much. This one, "Leadernomics," concentrates on leadership, and the sister book, "Going Agile," concentrates on agile management, particularly agile project management.

Here's a question for you - If things are going to go down the plug hole, how do we get ourselves out?

As it says in almost every good book on economics, there are only three ways to get out of a stagnating economic mess, you can:

1. Cut government spending massively (the quickest, but unless your name is Javier Milei, unlikely any politicians will ever pick it because it is so savage).

2. Miraculously and suddenly become massively more productive in the private in order to make the economy grow.

3. Some kind of mixture of the two (and it is incredibly hard to get the mix just right and really easy to get it badly wrong).

Personally, I think it's highly unlikely that option 1 or 3 are ever going to happen. But the great thing about option 2 is that we don't have to rely on the government to save us in order to make a difference to us.

You and I can do our bit to make things better.

It is up to us - that is, you and I. Not big global companies, and not big government. Actually, it always has been like that, and it always will be. It will be just up to people like us. It was the same for your great, great grandparents who started and built all the private mortgage companies, private health funds, private insurance funds, private local libraries and private pension funds before government took them over.

Their great, great, grandchildren can rebuild it all again - from nothing if needs be. (That's you and I).

The more productive we and the people we work with can become, the safer the jobs that our people and our co-workers will enjoy. And, with good fortune, as you grow in your enterprise the more jobs you can create for more people as we all become more successful.

* * *

And that is the reason why I wrote Leadernomics.

Let's Make A Start - What is Leadership?

W.C.H. Prentice gave us a classic definition of what leadership is, all the way in 1961. He said it is:

"the accomplishment of a goal through the direction of human assistants"[2] -

Not bad at all. I put his quote for two reasons:

1. It's a great start. It's a concise, practical working definition of what leadership is. We can work with it and we can keep it in mind for the rest of the chapter.
2. He was probably the very first person to say that leadership was more than just the result of possessing the physical power to be able to give someone a good kicking, or being so much extraordinarily smarter than everybody else around.

W.C.H. Prentice's article, "Understanding Leadership" is a brilliant article. It is available online and I urge you to read it. You will learn more about leadership in it's seven pages than in a bucket of other leadership books. But it raises it's own questions.

How do we actually direct the human assistants to accomplish the goal?

At this point, most books take some notes from some academics on what leadership is.. But the thing is, most academics couldn't lead a dog to their dinner, so what do they really know?

We need something a bit less academic. We need to know what does leadership actually mean in a practical sense?

---

[2] "Understanding Leadership" W.C.H. Prentice Harvard Business Review 1961

* * *

It means the ability to enthuse, inspire and encourage others to follow you on some kind of quest. Give them a great reason why they should do something and they will follow you. You won't need to push them - they will follow.

As far as we at Scrumnastics are concerned, that quest would be some kind of business project, but it needn't be limited to that at all. It could be anything.

Leadership is a mostly transferable skill. The leader of a group of builders could just as well be the leader of a football team, a social club, or a local political movement.

To us, leadership does NOT mean the ability to coerce, bully or force people to do as you wish. For the avoidance of doubt, we call this tyranny. We are against tyranny, and we are against that type of 'leadership' (even though it is probably the most common form of 'leadership' there is in the business world (and we have all been subject to it at some time or other in work, haven't we?).

Where does leadership come from?

Two ways: It is either imposed from above or it arises "organically." (That means people just emerge naturally). The essential components to it are:

1. Trust between you and your team

2. Your ability to raise the status of those in the team and high degree of status that the person is held in by the people they lead (we will talk about status elsewhere)

The practice of leadership emerges from taking the baby steps of normal people taking responsibility for making sure things get done over time. The people who do that get followed because they are trusted. That is where the seed of leadership germinates.

Reputations grow as time goes on. Other people will recognise that these people can be relied upon and so become more and more trusted, rather like a "virtuous spiral." This is the second part of leadership.

These various things that people first take responsibility for don't have to be large undertakings. They can be quite small, often trivial. In fact, it is often better if they are. After all, the last thing you need when you are beginning is a lot of pressure . Besides, isn't that how trust is built up? You are entrusted with small things and as people trust you they place more and more trust in you.

For example, when I was in school, everyone was encouraged from the earliest age to become responsible. From that we learned to lead.

It was drummed into us to "make ourselves useful," by every adult we had any dealings with. The assumption was that until we did, we were pretty useless and that was not a good thing to be.

At my school, very child over seven had a job to do. We weren't paid to do them, the payment was the increased status that being useful carried. The more useful you were, the greater status in the classroom you gained, and you became more highly valued.

It was how we learned the beginnings of responsibility. It was how we became trusted. You are probably the same.

There were all sorts of jobs like milk monitors, milk captains, pencil monitors, book monitors, school register monitors, school librarians, playground 'nurses' and a host of other small jobs that children could do and take responsibility for.

Every kid had a job for half a term and they got a different job every term. Repeat that every term until you were eleven and you became more and more responsible, trusted, and trusted to lead and the younger ones how to do the jobs you used to do.

Let me be clear: mine was not a posh school. It was a middling state school in a middling steel town on the border between England and Wales. - Trust me, as I have said elsewhere, Clytha Junior School was not Eton or Harrow.

* * *

Nevertheless, we all learned to be useful, and we all learned to become responsible. As we demonstrated we could work independently we became trusted by our classmates, teachers and the school.

So what does that tell us? It should tell us that leadership, or the beginnings of leadership, are not limited to superhuman posh boys and girls they are available to all, and from a very young age.

It also tells us that leadership can occur at many different levels - you don't have to want to be leader of the known universe and I think that is something that has been lost - we have been left with the impression that leadership only occurs from the top. Trust me, if you think that then you are going to be sadly disappointed.

This book, and we at Scrumnastics, aim at bringing back the idea that the natural state of affairs is that leadership is everywhere and can be done by almost everyone.

That kind of leadership is robust. The other is brittle and flakey.

"Leadership is not about being in charge. It is about taking care of those in your charge." Simon Sinek

Why do we need great leadership?

It's a tough question. Why bother? After all, look around, it's pretty obvious that many companies and organisations, especially in Britain, don't actually bother aspiring to great leadership. It's all a bit average, really, isn't it? But they're not actually going bust yet, are they? Are they?

Our problem is that traditional great leadership and great management have become replaced by administration, bureaucracy and something called "managerialism." (And you should know that mangerialism has very little to do with being a great manager, or even management).

We could try and struggle to come up with an answer but as well as the quote from President Ronald Reagan above, I am going to give you something from one of the greatest leadership and management gurus that most people have never heard of: William Edwards Deming.

"the aim of leadership should be to improve the performance of man and machine, to improve quality, to increase output, and simultaneously to bring pride of workmanship to people. Put in a negative way, the aim of leadership is not merely to find and record failures of men, but to remove the causes of failure: to help people to do a better job with less effort." — William Edwards Deming.

Great leadership can inspire, encourage, and enthuse a team of people to achieve things that they never thought they could, or were even possible.

With great leadership you can do more with fewer people and more rapidly. Even better, if you keep your existing staff numbers then they can do even more. You get greater capacity and greater capability. And that, my best beloved Leadernomist, affects the bottom line of your company because it will make you more profitable.

Great leadership can electrify a group of people. Bad leadership makes it seem as though they have been electrocuted.

But there is a much more down to earth reason: well led teams largely manage themselves, show more enthusiams for their work, show more initiative, are more content, work better, quicker, more intelligently and to a higher standard than badly led teams. - Which means that *your* day job becomes easier.

We do it to give our people a sense of belonging - that they are part of something bigger than just them

But why should you (or they) want to do that? -

Because we are social creatures. We have evolved to be social creatures becaue it is one of the secrets of success for human beings. By ourselves we are laughably puny, but in a group we are apex predators.

As social creatures we crave increased status from our peers. We also work better when we belong to a "tribe," even if its only a 9 to 5, Monday to Friday work tribe. People who feel they are not just a number belong to something bigger than them can go on to do extraordinary things.

How do you convince them of that? By raising their status by giving them a greater sense of identity and purpose than they would otherwise have. We will talk about how we do that later.

What makes our people feel as though they are part of something worthwhile?

We need to give them a reason '*why*' they are doing something. When learning, all adults like to know why they are doing something, it motivates them.

* * *

A strong, believable reason 'why' you and they are working towards achieving something better together gives greater clarity to everyone and everything you and your team will undertake, and that's a rare but good thing.

As Friedrich Nietsche said, **"Man can endure many hows with a strong enough why."**

In other words, if you and your people have an objective that is bigger than the inevitable hurdles that will crop up as you go along, so you will all overcome and get over them together.

A good reason why also gives you and your team an emotional and spiritual stamina that gets you successfully through those soggy, cold, clammy Wednesdays in February of the sould that we all have to go through in order to get to success.

With a good reason why your team should gain the ability to prioritise things more easily. The hard task of putting jobs in the right order so as to to get everything done most efficiently becomes a lot easier.

Priorities just become more obvious.

A good reason why also gives all of you greater clarity - clarity always reduces confusion within the team. Confusion is always wasteful and expensive. After all, labour costs are the most expensive component of any business, so the less your team spends in confusion and the more in clarity the better.

Or, you could just...

Well, instead of going to all of the trouble of the above you could always just shout at your people. After all, many companies do just that.

Worse, many companies and organisations have that as part of their management culture, don't they? I'm not joking, even today, machismo shouting and bullying is probably the most widely used management 'strategy' there is in Britain, France and America.

If that is the case, why should you change?

Easy: Fear and resentment creeping into a team is enormously hard to get rid of. It breeds suspicion. If you want to make any team underperform then all you have to do is just shout, bully and make them resentful. Sooner or later they will respond - you will see them slowly sabotage your best efforts.

They may not go so far as to actually throw a clog in the machine, but the slow sabotage will show up in small ways at first - they will work slower than they can - they will 'misunderstand' instructions - and worst of all, the best of them will look for jobs elsewhere, leaving you with the rump of your workers.

If you are lucky then you will still have enough money to be able to get someone like me to turn things around.

If you're unlucky then the very best of your team will leave, because good people ALWAYS have options, leaving you with the less talented members of your team.

And if you're really, really unlucky, then those good people with talent will create a brand new company to compete with you.

Good luck if that happens. I have worked with a load of wonderful, fresh, innovative, wildly successful companies that only started because they couldn't stand the old work culture, the boss of their old company or felt stifled working in it.

Okay, so we know why we should go to all the bother: great er capacity, greater capability and greater productivity. It gives us a better product or service that we can make quicker, at a higher quality, and cheaper than your competitors (who, lucky for you, are probably shouting even more at their people).

That gives you a real competitive advantage, which is a good thing in itself. But there's a second reason: that better, higher quality product or service that your team produces can now is more valuable. It will be able to command a higher price than you are charging now, which allows you to move up market.

Trust me, moving up market is now, and will be in the future, crucial to your business.

A huge amount of what we do now is getting our client companies to move upmarket.

Why move upmarket? Well, as Willie Sutton, the twentieth century bank robber said when he was asked why he robbed banks.

"Because that's where the money is."

But that's a topic for a different book.

Two Forms of leadership

To put it really crudely, the two major forms of leadership split down into:

1.   Top Down

2.   Bottom Up (also known as organic, or, as we call it, natural leadership)

Although they are meant to achieve the same thing, these two forms of leadership (and management) are very different from each other. **Top Down** is what we traditionally think of when it comes to leadership. It is the sort of thing that kings, generals, presidents, bureaucrats, technocrats, CEOs and business journalists like.

This is the environment where, ultimately, everyone in the chain of command gets their authority to do what they do from the very top person.

In the end, their authority comes from that top person having the ability to use some kind of force to enforce their authority, whether it is the threat of getting sacked or having, say, an army of people with swords or guns.

Bottom Up, or organic, or as we call it, "natural leadership," is when a leader just appears, or emerges, out of small, or small-ish groups. Bottom Up leadership is quite dynamic - it doesn't need buckets of rules, or bureaucracy because of its size. It is small enough that it doesn't need a lot of bureaucracy.

Imagine a bunch of small boys getting together spontaneously to play an impromptu game of football. The chances are that it will probably be led by two of the group who will just appear and step forward from the group. They will pick the teams, stick a few jumpers down for goalposts and then play. For what they are doing they really don't need the Football Association, do they?

When they get bored with the game and change to playing, say, cricket, it would more than likely be a different pair who choose who plays for which team.

Why choose bottom up?

It's possibly (probably?) the more natural way for human beings to organise themselves. After all, for millenia before we started farming, we were hunter gatherers in small-ish groups. For most of the time human beings have been on earth they have existed in small-ish groups, more tan likely based on the family. No need for complicated bureaucracy, or office politics, there.

There also seems to be a strange human trait that there is a maximum effective limit of around eleven people in a group. Around that size things are fairly simple to organise. You don't need lots and lots of rules to organise yourselves (ever wondered why team sports are mostly made up of eleven people in a side?).

Later, once you get to larger scale civilisations with things like farming and armies and navies, and kings and dukes and earls and things then you need more formal ways of organising yourselves, such as bureacracy.

But for most of us in the UK, the USA, Australia, New Zealand and Europe, we tend work well in small groups. I have worked in huge global companies and, guess what? Although the companies are huge they also tend to work on things in small-ish groups too, especially the really profitable ones.

And that is why we are concentrating on bottom up here.

But there is another reason…

When it is under stress, Top Down management can become really brittle very quickly and can break down easily. Conversely, bottom up tends to be more robust.

* * *

Why does it become brittle? Partly politics. I think it all comes down to wanting to be in a group, or rather, always wanting to be in the most important group. In a sense, that's what politics is all about.

I have seen this many, many times throughout my career as a management consultant. I think the reason is that although the executives at the top of a company may be officially leading and managing many hundreds of people, the group that they feel is most important is not the group of people they lead and manage, but the group of their peers.

Remember what we have said elsewhere in this book and also in this book's sister books: there is a very human tendency for us to only take the most serious notice of about eleven people.

When things get bigger than that it doesn't take long for office politics to emerge.

Consider that most human of things, a team sport. A football team has eleven people, a cricket team has eleven people and most team sports have teams of around eleven or less people in them. What is a team meant to do? Well, it's meant to win. When we want to win we have a tendency to form groups of eleven people or less.

As an example, in the 1970's and 1980s, there were all sorts of army revolutions in the world. Naturally, western governments were quite nervous about this and were pretty keen to find out whether they were vulnerable or not to this. As a result an organisation that was then called the "Stockholm Institute for Peace Research," were paid to do all sorts of research and surveys to find out what rank of army officer was likely to be responsible for staging successful coups. After all, it seemed like a useful thing to know if you were a nervous western government.

So, S.I.P.R.I went to work.

Were revolutions all generated by Generals, Admirals, or Air Commodores, for example?

Actually, no - these high ranking officers were far too high up, too busy doing politics to each other and so they were too disconnected from the service people who did the actual fighting.

They found that most successful coups in the world were started by the lower rank of army Colonels.

Why?

According to S.I.P.R.I., the rank of Colonel (or equivalent) was the highest rank that everyday soldiers had personal contact and some kind of relationship with. A General was too high and mighty, and too far removed from their life and their cares for them to care about or follow and joining a coup. They found that a Colonel was the highest rank where the officer could be expected to know the names of the individual soldiers that they commanded. This meant there was a personal bond that existed between the soldiers and their Colonels that did not exist between soldiers and their Generals

It seems that there is a point at which very "tall" hierarchies (having Generals, or Admirals) have a weak snapping point and are liable to break down. If the hierarchy gets too tall the common or garden people who actually do the work don't care that much about the top person in charge.

Also, as these vertical bonds become liable to snap, at the same time the horizontal bonds between the people in these 'elites' become a lot stronger - they look to each other more and more

It also seems that as time goes on, these vertical disconnections frequently open up between those at the middle and bottom of the hierarchy and those at the top who directly lead them. The connection is between the two ends can be brittle and become liable to snap or break.

This also happens in civilian life in companies and I have seen this many times. Once it begins to wear thin then the end seems inevitable and I have yet to see it successfully repaired anywhere.

We as leaders need to be aware of this because when it starts to appear it is definitely time to sharpen up your CV, or resume, and buy that previously annoying recruitment consultant a coffee or two and laugh at their terrible jokes.

Please note that this is   not just limited to old, past-their-best companies. I have seen this process of separation appear many times when working in businesses, particularly in hot-shot, new-ish businesses that have recently enjoyed meteoric success, - so please be warned.

It seems to start when the management team form a delusion and start to regard the companies success as being completely down to their own 'talent,' and not the efforts of the people underneath them who aqctually do all the work. You can always spot it by the way managers and directors talk to one another. They do a lot of joshing and socialising amongst themselves rather than with their staff. When this happens you can bet that the team is looking to each other rather than their people. This is where a culture of management delusion can form. Anyway, for now, just please be warned.

This managment delusion can generate all sorts of chaos. The number of times I have seen the workers get so fed up at the sometime appalling antics of the "management talent," (ranging from middle aged married men having affairs with staff, to directors skipping off work early, turning up at work with obvious hangovers, or even being intoxicated while at work).

What happens is that the workers rebel: they slowly begin to work less hard. Then, if left unchecked, they turn to very subtly sabotaging the company at an ever increasing pace.

This does not go unnoticed if there is a corporate owner of some kind. What happens is that the management team is swiftly decapitated and despatchedby the company's corporate owners.

They are often removed and replaced with another team the very same day.

That decapitation process of the whole top level of directors is not even that rare. Global corporations especially seem to have it written down as part of their playbooks and do it frequently. Did the 'management talent' deliver a really bad set of quarterly earnings for the second consecutive quarter? Been a bit "over friendly" with the crew? Then it can be goodbye, it's been average…

I hope you never come across it yourselves. I am really just putting it in here so you can take better care of yourself and your career.

But do be aware that this sort of thing has been around for hundreds of years. What other examples are there?

Well, when the Normans invaded England they literally decapitated all the Saxon nobles, left all the Saxon serfs on the land and put themselves in charge.

The French did the same during the French revolution. And the Russian Bolsheviks (a minority) killed all the Russian nobility during the Russian revolution.

So, unlike you, people who think to much of themselves at the expense of delivering results - people who think they are in 'the elites'? - They should remember to behave, do what they are supposed to do and play nice, all the time.

But that only tends to happen in Top Down organisations - you don't get that kind of thing with Bottom Up leadership.

That is probably because the bonds that tie people together in Bottom Up leadership are too close. There is just so much more interaction between people at lots of different levels. There are also a lot of leaders, like corporals and sergeants who all reinforce the rules of leadership.

Bottom Up leadership is more resilient than top down - it has so many people involved in it (both vertically and horizontally) that they all tend to bind to one another more strongly, and this tends to lend some self-correcting aspects. In other words, inevitable tension and even bad behaviour between each other is often sorted out in a more informal, though possibly more robust manner.

Which is something to think about - (probably before Bottom Up fans start chasing you with hammers and sickles).

So Why Should You Care?

So why should you care whether you are in a Top Down or Bottom up environment? Does it matter to you? Can you actually do anything about it?

After all, unless you are in a start up, you've probably just been promoted to the job you're in - you are in a Top Down environment, so why should you care about the other one?

Because the other type, the organic type, or Bottom Up, often just occurs spontaneously (but often separately) to the formal company organisation charts.

Leaders emerge, and sometimes they emerge behind your back - so watch out.

If you doubt it, have a look at what happened in the British car industry in the 1960s, 1970s, and 1980s. The management made a fatal mistake: they concentrated on management without paying attention to leadership. Nature abhors a vaccuum - so the shop stewards of the trades unions becamse the car workers leaders. Result? We don't really have a British car industry anymore.

Bottom Up structures are organic, this means that a parallel hierarchy can emerge and like I said above about the British car industry, it will not appear on any organisation chart.

It is important to realise how common these parallel authority structures can be. The mechanism that make them appear are old. Really old. As in older than humans have been around.

Even other mammals, like Chimpanzees, Gorrillas and even wolves and lions choose their leaders for their troupes in this organic, or Bottom Up way.

And remember, new or emerging leaders can emerge from nowhere. Next years leader may look very unimpressive this year. Be on your guard.

* * *

The good thing for you is that, if you take notice of what is in this book you won't have to worry because these parallel leaders only appears in a leadership vacuum.

Remember this: your people only want one leader and, if you are the official leader, you have a huge advantage over any potential challengers. In my experience, challengers only appear if the leader isn't very good, and if you have gone to the trouble of reading this book then that won't be you.

But what if we inherit a team where this has already happened? What do we do if you have inherited a team which has an already existing parallel organic structure? Can we combine the two?

How do you cope with that?

Easy. Subvert them by welcoming them and bringing them on side. Remember that to be an unofficial leader is an incredibly risky thing to be, so prove yourself to be a good leader and the competition will shortly evaporate.

That's the approach we use here at Scrumnastics and that is what we recommend.   Subvert them and bring them on side. You don't even have to be 100% successful at it. Just the sight of you attempting to bring them on side will often be often enough to bring their supporters onto your side - and that is all you really need to do.

 If we get to work in a larger company, we teach the client how to use Bottom Up leadership knowing that they are always going to continue with the Top Down.

The point is that knowing how to work with bottom up structures can pay benefits.

Besides, even the most hierarchical organisations can be made up of a mixture of the two.

Armies, navies, air forces, the police and fire services are normally a mixture of top down and bottom up structures. Obviously the commissioned officers are all in a top down environment but the soldiers, corporals, sergeants and sergeant majors are all in a bottom up environment.

It is worthwhile knowing the two.

What Is A Leader?

"A competent leader can get efficient service from poor troops, while on the contrary an incapable leader can demoralize the best of troops." - General John J. Pershing, U.S. Army

This section does not aim to turn you into another Winston Churchill, but it will try to stop you from becoming another little Hitler. After all, there was only one Winston Churchill, but as we know from the bosses we have all had in real life, there are an awful lot of little Hitlers around.

What Makes A Good Leader?

Trust. They trust you .They trust you to look after them. They trust that you will look after them and fight battles for them that they cannot fight - even if it is to your detriment.

The ability to **motivate** them. That means encouraging them both individually and collectively.

The ability to **raise their status**.

Of course, they also have skills and ways of thinking that you may not have at the moment. But that's fine, they are skills, and there is a section on them later on, so you can learn them.

Of course, you will have to practice the skills, and also the ways of thinking until you master them, but you can do it. It just takes a little study, some work and practice.

In some ways, learning leadership as a bit like learning to drive a car. When you pass the test and you get your licence it does not mean you are a great driver - it just means you are probably not actually a danger to others. The real skills of learning to drive comes after you have passed the test. It is the practice on different roads and different weather that makes you good. Experience beats a licence.

The media would have us believe that leaders are supermen and women, born to be leaders and somehow different to the likes of you and I.

But that's just business journalists for you, and most of them couldn't lead a kid into a sweet shop. All they do is fancy typing and they have never run anything, so what do they know?

This notion of leaders being super beings is simply nonsense. A nonsense built on stilts. Leaders are just normal human beings, just like you and me. In fact, they really are _exactly_ _like_ _you_ _and_ _I_, after all, despite the cliche, most _weren't_ born to be leaders.

What is a good leader? Someone with the skills, ways of thinking, vision and credibility that persuade people it will be worthwhile following them. In other words, as we have said before - they trust you to lead them.

Where do the vision and credibility come from? Credibility is part confidence, and that comes from the mastery of the skills and ways of thinking. The vision? There's a section on that later on.

Let's Get Down To It:

First things first: We are the leaders that we have been waiting for. No-one else is coming to save us. Sorry, there is no-one else. There's only us. Remember the quote from the beginning of this book from Colour Sergeant Bourne in the 1964 film, "Zulu."

You remember that boss that you worked for and that you couldn't stand because they were not up to the job? Well, unfortunately, they were only there because people like us didn't volunteer for the job _first_.

The first part of learning to be a leader is putting yourself forward to be a leader. And we have to.

* * *

If you don't put yourself forward for leadership then the clowns like your former boss get the job. And clowns are never funny. Bad leaders wreck individual lives and careers, the lives of teams and even companies.

In thirty years of consulting, I have seen it a hundred times or more. So, best-beloved Leadernomist, every time you roll your eyes, or sniff eloquently at the latest, brainless nonsense that came out of their mouth, think on this: they are only there because you didn't back yourself enough to go for the job.

It is time to step up.

For sure, as we embark on becoming a leader, we will have to do some hard work to hone our skills and transform who we are. Be careful: once we start, it leaves a mark just like a tattoo - and there is no going back. That honing work is like sharpening a blade: it carries on forever. Be sure that this is what you want.

You may be thinking, "But I can't do that, I'm not an 'alpha' personality type. Besides, I really like the job I have and I am good at it. How can I possibly lead a team?"

First of all, it sounds like you have fallen for the trap of 'leaders have to be super beings.'

Human beings don't have 'alpha' personalities. Actually, if you want to be technical, lions, chimps and gorillas do exhibit that personality type - Human beings don't. Why? Because when we became social beings it seems that all the beta males got fed up with the alpha males getting all the females so they all got together and killed the individual alpha males. They did this for generation upon generation until they went extinct.

Human beings no longer have alpha personalities So, if human beings don't have alpha personalities then you don't need to worry whether you have one or not, do you?

* * *

You can lead people and you will lead people. Actually, almost everyone can. I have mentored a lot of new leaders over the past 30 years, some of which have definitely started off as what silly journalists call beta type personalities. However, with some training, coaching, and mentoring, and a considerable effort on the part of the trainee, almost all turn into what a journalist would call an alpha personality.

While we are on the subject, in my experience, there's no such thing[3] as a fixed personality 'type,' there are just different behavioural habits which people move between.

For example, unless you are some kind of psychopath, I hope you probably behave in a completely different way with your parents than you do with your best friends on a night out.

We change our behaviour depending on the environment and company we find ourselves in - and we change a lot.

Which means you _**can**_ be a leader.

By the end of this section you will know enough to be in a position to credibly and confidently lead a small team with your team respecting you as their leader.

How? Because you will begin to know more about what people actually want and need from their leaders in order to motivate them to work at their very best. Knowing that, as far as it is possible, we can give that to them.

By the way, please don't get discouraged when I use the words "lead a small team." This is not a small thing. This is not small beer.

If you can lead a small team _then you can lead a large team too_. However, it doesn't necessarily work the other way around. Many 'leaders' of huge organisations can't lead small teams.

* * *

---

[3] I think this only exists in the minds of business journalists.

Leading a small team is actually harder than leading a large team. In small groups your people are looking very closely at you, every day.

In larger groups, people not only look at you, but they also take their cues from looking at everyone else around you who are also looking at you.

Many of those people in the large group will be giving lots of positive, non-verbal feedback that everyone will be picking up on.

Large groups of people self-reinforce everyone's beliefs. After all, there's a reason why it took so long to see the king had no clothes on.

This Is How They See You - So Why Should They Follow You?

You need to understand that the people you are trying to lead are people with hard-won, largely practical skills that they have invested money, time, hard-work and practice to acquire, and which they use to get paid.

And because of that, they won't have much respect for you when you start leading them. They literally think that they are useful and that you are useless.

As you are a leader or manager, their default view is to look at you as someone with no real skills at all. Think about that for a moment. They know they have skills because they get paid to use them but they think of you as completely unskilled (let's say it again, _useless_).

If you are having to be a leader on a part time basis (because you are also a person with (say) a trade) then they won't give you too much of a hard time. Why? Because almost everyone with a trade is by definition useful.

But if you are a full time leader then you are going to have a much harder time of it. They don't just think you are useless, but they know that your salary is coming out of the products of their hard work. They don't just see you as useless - they see you as a parasite.

Part of your job is to show them that there really are skills to leadership and management, that they don't have and that you have mastered. _More than that, when you employ those skills then they will see their working lives get better._

Do that and convince them that you have skills and you will be on your way. They will begin to respect you. Slowly, slowly, you will earn their trust.

They will realise that you are some_one_ worth following, because you will know how to give them some_thing_ worth following. It is entirely normal for people to want a positive return on their efforts isn't it? They want to be better off than they were yesterday and they want to be even better off tomorrow.

Offer them a good chance of being better off tomorrow than they are at the moment and there is an extremely good chance that they will follow you. Why? Because it is in their best interests to do so.

Just knowing this stuff will make you a better leader than the vast majority of leaders, especially those in Britain.

Sssshhhhhhh… Here's A Dirty Little Secret About Leadership. - Don't Tell Anyone.

Like I have already said elsewhere, leadership is essentially a craft, a bit like a trade, - just like the people you are probably going to be leading have.

Like all trades and crafts it requires a combination of some knowledge, some practical skills, a drop of talent and practice of that knowledge and these skills to get really good at it. Oh, and just remember: a certain amount of humility goes a very long way.

* * *

As one of my mentors told me when I was a very young man, "Lead with humility, it may stop you from getting completely humiliated in front of your people."

Leadership is definitely not something that only certain special people are just born to do. Like all craftwork, once you have mastered some fairly simple skills you can only get better and better at it by doing it over and over. We will study the skills as we go but before we do, let's deal with hierarchies.

First of all, despite what some may say, there are such things as groups and hierarchies. - And we need to deal with that.

The first thing that is on your side is to know that almost everyone wants and needs to be in a group - because you have greater status being in a group than you do as an isolated individual. It probably goes back to when we were hunter gatherers. To be in a group meant you probably ate and prospered, whereas to be alone meant you were likely to be eaten.

You may not believe that there are such things as hierarchies and you may not like them, but whether you do or not is immaterial. The only people who will tell you there is no such thing as a hierarchy are those in the middle or at the bottom of a hierarchy.

They do this because it makes them feel better because they know they are at the middle or the bottom of a hierachy.

Obviously, as a leader, you will be at the top of the hierarchy of the group you are leading. Many bad leaders think that you get to the top of a hierarchy by appearing to being the strongest, and so they strut about, they posture, and behave accordingly. This is a terrible tactic because the people in the team see this. You might as well put a target on your back.

This is a completely and utterly wrong approach. You actually get to the top and stay at the top of any hierarchy by being the best and most competent at what you do.

Here's a question: Let's pretend for a moment that you run a really great house building company. It is the very best for miles around and customers flock to you. Do you get to be a really good house building company by being excellent at project, time and cost management, knowing where to source the finest materials, seeking out the best crafts people, and running excellent teams, or because you are an strutting, rutting "alpha" male or female?

It is not a trick question, is it?

It is the same with leadership and management. You get to be the best leader and manager by studying, practicing, and mastering skills and then mastering yourself.

Here's the amazing thing that automatically puts you light years ahead of other leaders and managers: most of them don't bother learning about leadership and management and would rather strut around striking power postures instead.

As Forrest Gump's mother said in the film, "stupid is, as stupid does." But not you, dear best beloved Leadernomist, Not you.

What Makes A Leader A Leader?

Despite what you might read in newspapers, websites and business magazines, leadership has little to do with being a charismatic and domineering personality or a self-important extravert. That is just public relations.

When needed, a leader will emerge with no regard to the company organisation chart because they are already there and people look to them already. Because they are trustworthy.

And if you are working in a larger company where the formal organisation structure doesn't have a space for the natural leaders in it, when a crisis hits the organisation will be all over bar the shouting.

Why? Because natural leaders have their leadership entrusted to them by the people - not the HR department.

* * *

Trust me, I have seen it dozens of times, in a tussle between the people and the "HR Business Partners," the people win. Every time.

Leadership stems from a peculiar mix of the right social skills, not formal authority. You do not grab it - your people , the people around you, grant it to you.

A leader is someone who has character and a knowledge of those few skills and behaves in a way that their people look toward for support or direction when they need to. Such leaders are always needed, and this is what makes people _want_ to follow them, in good times and bad, towards a vision or set of goals.

But why do people follow them? Among other reasons, because they

1. Know _**what**_ they are doing - They are competent - and as we know, not everyone in a position of leadership is.

2. They know _**why**_ they are doing it - they have a compelling 'reason why.' Again, most leaders and managers don't.

3. They know _**where**_ they are going - They have a compelling vision of a worthwhile goal that appeals to others.

4. They know _**how**_ they are going to get there - They know how to successfully organise people, money and things, have mastery at least one form of management and have a working knowledge of others

5. They know _**who**_ they can take with them, and what those people want.

In addition, they must also have some old-fashioned character traits like 'presence' and 'heft.' With those comes respect for you.

Old fashioned virtues lend respect. Amongst other traits, leaders must also be emotionally strong and brave, honest, and reliable, behave with integrity and be able to champion their people in front of others.

One other dark thing about respect. The other reason you will earn respect that that it will be obvious that you are potentially dangerous. Do not be a pushover. Stand your ground when challenged. It is a test: the people who will challenge expect you to assert yourself. You don't have to be phyical. A snake does not bite everything it encounters - a simple hiss does the trick more often than not. But do remember to hiss.

Also, people want a moral dimension from their leaders. Nobody follows anyone for long when they behave inappropriately like having affairs, turning up drunk, or behaving inappropriately with staff.

Get those things right and you have cracked it... By the way, although I said leadership was simple, I didn't say it was easy.

For example: Nuclear fusion is essentially simple - jam two hydrogen atoms together and fuse them which will release enormous but it is definitely not easy.

Words From A True Leader:

Here are some words to ponder from an interview of Field Marshall Montgomery, who defeated General Rommel in North Africa during the Second World War. He then commanded more than **_two million men_** during the Allied invasion of Europe via Normandy. **_Two million men_**. Now, that's someone who knows about leadership.

Lord Stephen Taylor: "As you look round the world today, Field Marshall, do you see the need for leadership, still?"

Viscount Montgomery: "Oh, terribly. Terribly. And I see it in industry, I think that many of the problems that go on in the world today are due to the bad leadership on the parts of the people in high places."

But won't be you, best beloved Leadernomist. Not you.

Managerialism

This is the bane of public sector. It basically means people with the job title of manager but without the capability to manage.

There's a very old cliche that says, "if it walks like a duck, swims like a duck and quacks like a duck, then it's probably a duck." Sounds perfectly reasonable, doesn't it? It is a good working assumption. Of course, the problem with assumptions is that they don't always apply.

It's the same with what passes for some forms of management

There are an awful lot of jobs in the world of companies and organisations with very important sounding job titles which seem like management jobs but which aren't. - These are the administrative jobs. And these are the "Managerialist" jobs

Those involved in Managerialism don't see themselves as simply doing a job, rather, they see themselves as belonging to a group. There are hundreds of thousands of people in these jobs in the U.K., so many that they form their own little mini class.

If there is one phrase that they could all agree on then it would be: "We konw better than you."

That was bad enough but then as time has gone by it has expanded into an ideology defined as: Management + Ideology + Expansion = Managerialism.

"Managerialism combines management knowledge and ideology to establish itself systemically in organisations and society while depriving owners, employees (organisational-economical) and civil society (social-political) of all decision-making powers. Managerialism justifies the application of managerial techniques to all areas of society on the grounds of superior ideology, expert training, and the exclusive possession of managerial knowledge necessary to efficiently run corporations and societies."

Thomas Klikauer in "Managerialism – Critique of an Ideology"

(2013)

Many of them would describe themselves as "the elites."

But not me. Full disclosure: I loathe these people, their attitudes and their fake air of competence. And I loathe them because I am convinced that they the true useless eaters in our society. They are a drain on the productivity of this country.

I believe management done well is a noble calling. Study Japanese companies such as Toyota, Honda, Yamaha and Panasonic and you will learn just how great the Japanese are at management. It is one of the secrets behind their international success.

There is such a thing as the power paradox. There are those who are attracted and apply for a position because they want the prestige even when they do not have the ability to do it. The problem with the power paradox is that those people are attracted often don't know anything about management. To the extent that they rely on eminence not evidence

Managerialism - is the Enemy of Great Leadership

THE MOST IMPORTANT TOPIC IN THIS BOOK

Status And How We Deal With It

Status. We all need a measure of it to thrive. That's just common sense, really isn't it? After all, status gives us confidence and it's very pleasant to feel confident, isn't it?

To be an isolated, lone individual is to have little or no status apart from what they give themselves, and that doesn't really count. To be in a group is to have a lot more status, partly because we are in the group, and partly because our colleagues also give us status. However, once we are in a group our problems aren't over. It is then that we enter a constant, day in, day out competition to gain more status and hopefully rise up in the ranks.

There are always high status people in groups and there are always lower status people in groups. Some people obviously need more than others but to a lesser or greater extent all of us need it. And that need is voracious because the "hit" that status gives is always temporary - it wears off - and it wears off quickly.

Bought a new car? You'll probably get loads of status from that feeling of achievement of picking it up, owning it, and all the admiration from the onlookers. However, get involved in an accident 30 meters from the garage you just picked it up from and get it all bashed up? - All or part of that status disappears immediately. Ephemeral stuff, status.

It's a big thing too, status. The latest research tells us that money is nothing more than a stand-in for status. Apparently, we don't work for money, we work for the status that the money represents. So for all you who work for companies who employ contractors and only reward them with money? - Think again if you treat them as glorified wage slaves. The competitor who treats them with dignity will capture them from you.

Are you still convinced that just giving money is all you need to do? Have you ever been in the company of the "genteel poor"? There are loads of them in Britain. They are the ones who may be financially poor now, but five generations back they were aristocratic and loaded.

Betray your lack of breeding in front of them and they can rob you of your status and elevate themselves above you with nothing more than an eloquent sniff. or a raised eyebrow.

Status. Understanding it can give us another set of tools that others are not aware of.

This is probably the most important topic in this book. Get this right and you have cracked leadership - the rest is simply tactical tools and techniques. As we know, tools can be very handy but know-how trumps everything. Know about status and you know about just about everything in the human world and how to achieve it.

In fact, if the latest research that has recently uncovered about human beings and status really is true, status and how we deal with it may be the most important subject ANY of us ever read about EVER.

I think it will soon also change every book on leadership. The reason is simple: status determines how we interact with each other in everything we do. It is fundamental.

What is weird is that although the research is incredibly new, what it talks about is ancient.

You may have read Jordan Peterson's book, "Twelve Rules For Life." One of the chapters of his book talks about lobsters and how they are almost entirely driven by status and seeking more of it. Why? Well, the more status you have, the bigger you get to grow and the more offspring you get to make.

When I read about it I thought "Yeah, but that's just for lobsters, we are far more sophisticated."

As it turns out, I completely wrong. We really, really aren't much more sophisticated. The latest research shows that that chapter in Peterson's book probably understates what a fundamental impact status and our never ending hunt for more and more of it has on all our lives - all the time.

Did you know that we constantly gauge each other's status? We even have a part of our brain that is dedicated to it.

We do it every day and every hour. We can look at a stranger and tell immediately where they are in our particular hierarchy, where we are in that hierarchy, and where we are in relation to them in that hierarchy. Amazing eh? Oh, and we can do all that gauging and sizing up in one tenth of a second - it is hard wired into us.

In fact the mechanism we use to sum each other up and gauge each other is contained in a very old and very special part of the brain that we share with all animals higher on the evolutionary ladder than a lobster. In other words, every vertebrate under the sun has this.

Which means it is also hard wired into other animals such as chimpanzees, gorillas, dogs, lions, all other mammals and all the way back down the evolutionary tree going all the way back to lobsters.

How old? This mechanism developed and has been working since before lungs and skin appreared on planet earth. It is that old.

Knowing about this stuff (and being able to use it) will make a huge difference to your success as a leader. In fact, I think it will make a huge difference to your success in life.

Obviously, we are going to study it from the pont of view of being better leaders, but once you understand the basics you will understand and solve all sorts of situations around you that mystify others.

Ever watched two managers 'debate' with one another where you know that both their arguments are completely wrong? You might see it and think, "That's simply mad. Why on earth are they doing that?" What you are seeing is not a battle for getting to the truth, or a battle to get to the best solution for all concerned. It is simply a battle for status.

I know this from my own work life. At one time, I was a data architect. My job was to analyse a company's customer, product and sales data and show the directors where they should concentrate to give their huge, global company the very best future. Sometimes I presented my findings and I would be mystified at their flat refusal to even entertain what I had shown them. Why did they refuse to listen?

Simple: status. They were all twenty years older than me, had very expensive business degrees, had lucrative and successful multi-decade careers and so, despite my facts and figures, they listened to each other and wouldn't listen to me.

Now it didn't matter to me because I got paid whether they took notice of my findings or not. I got my status from being able to pay to put my children through private school.

And that's a real problem that we need to pay attention to as leaders who inevitably have to deal with other leaders: just because your colleagues have high status doesn't always mean they are right, or competent.

Although status and competency CAN, and often do go hand in hand, they don't necessarily have to.

Status: the four rules of status

In order for someone to raise their status, there are four rules that have to be followed in order or it to work.

1. In order to receive higher status, we have to feel as though we are somehow deserving of higher status.

2. To truly gain status it must be done in public in the eyes of others. It is a bit like justice, it must be seen to be done. Your higher status is conferred by your peers.

3. The person has to have some measure of status already. Attempting to raise the status of the lowliest in a group by a large amount in one step simply does not work because the people around them will not accept it. If you are to be sucessful in raising status really high then it must be done in stages.

4. Rejection of any reluctance to claim status. In other words, in order to gain status you have to be open to gaining higher status. To the ambitious, this may sound odd, but there are many personalities (often referred to these days as "sigma" personalities, but when I was a kid they were simply called "loners") who reject the outright pursuit of

status. Frankly, they would really rather not bother with what they see as a tiresome game.

First Understanding:

If you are going to be aware of using status then you have to accept the following: there is a basic assumption that we are almost entirely driven by the voracious and insatiable need for status. We can also have completely different levels of status in different environments. Status can also quickly evaporate to nothing - just like that.

Just because we may be in a high status place in this environment, it doesn't follow that we are in another. Being a champion darts player doesn't necessarily mean you are also a champion footballer.

Second Understanding:

There are many currencies in our world, not just cash. All currencies are used as a means to exchange things, and some of those things can be very subtle indeed. We may think that money is the only route to high status, but long before there was money there was status. In many walks of life, the distinction between the two has grown a bit fuzzy. In fact, money has become a way of measuring status, hasn't it? The more money you have the greater your status. But, and this bit is important, money is actually only a proxy for status - it has not completely replaced it and it never will. Most important, those who enjoy very high status may not have much money to hand but they will never let you forget who has the higher social standing.

If you think of those organisations where the pay is not that great, such as the civil service, or universities and their lecturers, people compete to be top dog by using prestige, or virtue rather than showing off their paychecks and what they can buy. Don't forget the sniffy attitude of those snobby, genteel poor we mentioned above who see anyone with a lot of money showing off as being beneath them - rather uncouth and "common," dahling. They achieve their hit of status by looking down their noses and feeling superior. We call them the status vampires, or status parasites.

Why am I talking about money as a substitute for status? Well, many business owners and managers have a very money oriented (remember me talking about "Theory X" managers?) view of how they should reward their staff and the above illustrates that, as leaders and managers who strive to be the best, we should not be so one dimensional. How? Give your people credit. It is amazing how incredibly and rapidly transformative some encouraging words can be - and it's completely free, too.

So we now know that status is generally probably more important than we gave it credit for, and we will tend to pay it more attention, but what do we need to know about it as leaders?

Well, status affects us and our teams. For someone to be part of a team adds to their status. They now belong to something, even if they are at the bottom of the pack for the moment. Whereas before? They didn't exist in their colleagues' eyes..

We are social creatures. Being social creatures who work very well together is probably one of the reasons that we have become the dominant species on the planet. After all, in comparison to a lion, a tiger or a bear we are puny. But acting together we can overcome them all.

Also, being a part of a tribe or a team means we are accepted as being useful, and that in itself raises our status.

Now, not being part of a tribe or team might be for a very good reason - we may, in fact, be useless, and being useless can invite open contempt from others. If we carry on then we may become shunned. One of the worst things that can happen to us is to become outcasts, or isolated, or excommunicated, or socially cancelled. In the days when we were a hunter gatherer, then being made an outcast would be the equivalent of a death sentence.

On the other hand, when you are part of a team or tribe it probably means you are useful and are valuable to that team. You get to eat.

As you know, my colleagues and I are an Agile project manager consultancy, mostly in the digital world, but also in a very wide set of industries. We teach people to work together in a better, more productive way. In doig that we often have to create completely new teams from scratch with people who have never worked together before. Whenever I have to do that, I spend a lot of effort building a sense of camaraderie, or team spirit amongst them. Why do I bother? Because it works.

I start by giving the individuals en<u>cour</u>agement. The "cour" in the word "encouragement" is taken from the old Norman French word for heart, or "coeur." Therefore, to encourage someone is to literally give them more heart.

Conversely, to discourage someone is to take heart from them, or demoralise them. I see lots of weak leaders and managers who are so unconfident of their abiities that the way in which they manage their people is to discourage them by making them feel bad. - But not you, of course. Not you.

Why do I do it? Because it works. Elevating the status of our people pays dividends for them and me - they work quicker, and better than a bunch of discouraged individuals.

But what about us, the leaders?

We also need a certain amount of status in order to confidently lead a team, and the people in our teams need to see that we possess a certain amount of status too, before they add to your status. Here's the trick: your status should be higher than theirs, but not <u>too</u> much higher than theirs. Too much higher and the gap in status between you and them will start to breed resentment against you, and, sooner or later, resentment will bring about sabotage.

Honesty time: let's be frank, at least part of the reason that we become leaders is for the added status that that brings to us - and there's nothing wrong with that, it is one of the fuels for ambition, and it is good to be ambitious.

So What Are The Things That Will Give Us Status?

Although there may be more, the research says that there are three main pathways to getting more or higher status. The first one we can't really affect in any way but the second and third types have a direct bearing on us. The three types are:

1.   Demand, or Dominance. - Status is demanded of you. This can give the person receiving it potentially the highest possible status of the three types. How do they get it? Someone can demand that their people give them status through possessing some kind of dominance, like being a king or a president. We willingly give status to a king, or a president partly through habit but also because we know they probably have many thousands of very rough men behind them armed with very sharp pointy things or very effective shooty things. In other words, we give them status because there is an underlying threat of violence behind them and, being wise, we defer to them.

Once we understand that there is some kind of underlying or background violence in the mix then it is easy to understand that we can add warlords, mafias,and drug cartels and gangs to the list. For the vast majority of the time, hopefully, we can avoid dealing with these types. Of course, mafia dons and warlords don't often get to enjoy their retirement and their grandchildren, so I think it's for the best if we try and avoid that one.

2. Prestige. - Prestige mostly gives less status than demand, but not always. It always delivers more than virtue. We gain prestige by demonstrating, or having demonstrated, some kind of success. It is precisely this success, delivered in front of some kind of audience that increases our status in the group. The prestigious person will have demonstrated real expertise and probably over a good length of time.

It is easy to see this in sports television. Who do we get to commentate on big sporting games to lead us through a televised match? Well, getting someone who was an outstanding player during their professional career and can also string a few words together is probably a good start. Definitely more interesting and a better bet than getting Colin in accounts to offer their opinions on the telly on the big game.

Of course, that prestige has to be real and authentic. One thing we have to make sure of and look out for is to weed out those people who fake their success and prestige, and, sad to say, there are more and more of those. When I say fake, I'm thinking of all sorts of things such as fake qualifications, to deliberately putting fake jobs on their CVs, but any kind of fakery is fakery. Beware especially of those that indulge in what soldiers call "stolen valour," which boils down to pretending you did something when you did not. Luckily, the great thing about real expertise (the kind that comes from experience) is that it is mostly easy to recognise as it carries a certain amount of fame and reputation which goes with the person. If I was a hippy (which I am not) I would call it their 'aura.'

Of course, prestige can also be gained many more mundane ways, like doing a job well, or achieving success while being a part of a group of people . In reality, most of the prestige we gain is through work - You don't have to have been a rock star or a premier divison captain in a former life to obtain pestige - hard work, a bit of talent and 'stickability' (tenacity and perseverence) more than do the trick.

3. Virtue - Virtue is the most problematic of the three. Virtue offers the least amount of status of the three when people indulge in it and can often be the most problematic, mostly because it is the easiest to fake. As you might imagine, using this method you gain status by being virtuous, whatever that may mean. You may gain it by holding views that are highly moral, or highly modern or liberal. On the other hand, depending on the situation or environment, you might appear virtuous by demonstrating very traditional virtues indeed. One man's or woman's virtue can be another man's immorality.

The biggest problem with virtue is that it is not prestige. The reason prestige works is that prestige comes from being able to demonstrate a practical thing, skill, or craft. Virtue? That's largely about being nice.

Your prestige could come from being a champion sports person or being an exquisite woodworker, or metal worker or the very best sales person in the company. Being the nicest person I know might not cut it in the real world or in the sight of your colleagues and will definitely not give you as much status in their eyes.

The other problem that depending upon virtue to get your hit of status is what we now call virtue signalling. Crudely put, it is the attempt to gain status or kudos by professing, and even attempting to extend certain group standards.

Its not up to me to tell you one way or the other but it is up to me to tell you that we all need a certain amount of positive status to thrive. And having some of the people that you need to lead relying on the poorest returning method of gaining status is not optimal for you, your team or them.

Because virtue signalling gives such poor returns, those that rely on it have to spend a lot of time working at it to get their fix instead of getting on with working productively and getting their fix from achieving greater prestige.

So what is the solution to having a bunch of virtue signallers in the team that you may be leading? Practical skills. Give them practical skills or a pathway to achieve practical skills that have status in the eyes of their colleagues. It will take time but it will work for most of them.

A "Sideways Look" At Understanding Status

Which came first, status or money? Well, if we accept that mammals use status in their groups, it has to be that status came first, right? Status seems to be money's ancestor. But these days it seems that money has become a stand in for status. Status is also similar to money in that it can also be thought of, and also used as, a currency. You can earn status, you can spend status (wisely or foolishly) and you can be robbed of your status. Your status, just like money, can go up and down. Take enough away in an abrupt way and few will ever recover.

It can also suffer from inflation and debasement with over use, so be careful in how you share it around in your team and how you spend it. Be judicious - it makes it all the more valuable when you give it.

So How Do We Generate Status for those in our team?

The easiest way to elevate someone's status is to give them some encouragement in front of their peers. A quick "what an excellent piece of work," or suchlike to the person responsible for an achievement in front of all their colleagues can have a remarkable and lasting effect.

Of course, you need to make sure that the reason for the encouragement is truly warranted - because it needs to be sincere - but encouragement works wonders. I used not much more than encouragement when I took over a failing team and they doubled the amount of work they produced in six weeks and became the top team in the organisation. I think I was moe astonished than they were. Anyway, I now use it all the time when building or rebuilding a team and, as I have just said, have had spectacular results in productivity over a short period of time.

You also have to make sure that over time, each individual in the team receives some encouragement. Of course, encouragement needs to be given in a careful judicious way because if you over use it it will become devalued very quickly.

What diminishes, attacks or destroys status?

Broadly speaking, it comes down to negative attacks on a person's character or reputation. Things such as humiliation, character assassination and discouragement (which is the most widely used, especially by bad managers). All of these affect the quality and amount of work someone will do.

Being humiliated in front of your colleagues is now seen by researchers as being incredibly (and sometimes permanently) damaging, so let's leave that to the bad leaders.

These same researchers now see humiliation as having an immensely negative effect on status. It has even been defined as "an annihilation of the self" by the researcher James Gilligan and even as "the nuclear bomb of the emotions."

These same people have a possibly different definition of shame. They define shame as the version of humiliation that happens in private, when there are no witnesses. Although it is not quite as damaging as humiliation, sometimes it is not far off.

* * *

With such strong, powerful descriptions of what humiliation and shame can do to someone, and how it can affect their work performance, why is it that so many leaders and managers still use humiliation and shame as techniques for leading and managing people? It is counter productive isn't it?

Yet even now, in the end of the first quarter of the twenty-first century, we still see loud echoes of the old split between the"Theory X" and "Theory Y" manager as written about in Douglas Magregor's 1960 book, "The Human Side Of Enterprise."

At one time, this book was on the reading list of every management course in the land. Unfortunately, the book and the study of it seem to have fallen out of fashion. Will we soon find from the new research on status that bad productivity and failing companies have little to do with the skill and arts of leadership and management but just having too many of a certain type of personality abusing their power in order to get a hit of status in order to boost their ego? I have my own suspicions, I am sure you do too.

Watch Out For Office Politics...

If you are working in a large companyor organisation (meaning that there's a lot of office politics going on,) you need to be aware of how widely status can be used by your colleagues at the same level or higher than you to destabilise both your, and your teams good work.

Luckily, all of us have a what I call a built in "status weather glass." What is it? It's our posture. Feeling full of confidence? You naturally stand up tall. Had a row with your significant other? Now you won't stand quite so tall.

I need you to begin to become aware of your posture and how it can change throughout the day. Start this in the morning. Get up and go to the bathroom, look in the mirror, stand up as tall as you can, pull your shoulders back and give youself a mark out of ten (hopefully ten). Whenever you have some kind of interaction with anyone then check yourself and remark how you feel, again out of ten.

If you feel a bit low then make a conscious effort pull your shoulders back and stand up as tall as you were this morning. Get used to this and make this into a habit. It is a great simple tool that will serve you well. It is such a good tool that I also teach this to the people in my teams.

Armed with this new tool in your workplace, you need to begin to become make a mental note of any snide comments that come from those in work who are not necessarily close to you and your team. Again, as these things inevitably happen, become aware of any changes that happen to your body posture.. Remember: check and rebalance yourself by making your posture what it should be.

The check is easy: make sure you pull your shoulders back and stand up tall and remark yourself out of ten.

This is going to happen to you, because it happens to all of us, but when it does, you will no longer need to make any immediate response. Imagine that. You don't have to come up with some witty retort, you just need to stand up straight and tall.

Why? Because anyone who plays the status game will be looking to see if your posture has changed as a result of their actions. The reason they do it is to dominate you and they will always want to see if their actions have worked. But standing up straight and tall and looking them straight back in the eye is the very best revenge, because they will see that their efforts have not worked.

Even better, they have just shown you their hand while you kept quiet and you did not show yours. Let your team's successes speak for themselves - and while you are about it, do remember to teach the body posture trick (and the reasons why they should do it,) to your team. It will work wonders in their work life and also their lives outside.

If you are curious enough to want to know more about the wider subject of status, a great place to start is Will Storr's book **"The Status Game."** It really is a very good book to start with, it is well researched and he also cites the names of those who have actually done all the original research, which provides you with a wide variety of jumping off points so you can do a lot more deeper research should you want to. I believe there is also an Audible version of it if you prefer.

Obviously, we have only had time to skim the surface of this new research here. However, even the little that I have outlined in this section is a core part of how we work. Why do we spend time on it? Because raising the status of those in our teams works. I mean it really works. It is quite common for people outside of our teams to remark on the positive change in attitude, confidence and pace that our teams work at.

It is one of our secret sauces that make our projects hit their agreed dates and deliver on time, every time. And now you can use it too.

I feel my team are judging me…

You bet they are! Of course they are. Every day. You are right - you are not suffering from paranoia. They are judging you, and they are doing it every day and possibly after every interaction within a day that they see you have.

Yesterday, today, and tomorrow.

And it is inevitable that they do that. They have to. - And they have every right to do so.

Part of the reason is that they will be checking whether they can still trust you to lead them today. They have to do this. They have no option. Why? Their positions are precarious by their very nature. There are of course many other reasons but partly because as their leader you are their protector against an onslaught from other teams. So the question that has to be going through their minds every day is, "am I still on a winning team and are you still strong enough to protect me?" Let's also not forget that they are looking at you because you have power over them.

So what are they judging? Everything! Things like, what is your mood like today? Positive? Negative? How should we respond to that? Are your moods always on an even keel or have you been liable to fly off the handle lately? They will be wondering why that is because it affects them directly.

How is your health? Are you fit and strong today? Are you fitter and stronger than yesterday or are you weaker? How will you defend them by speaking truth to power if you are not at your best? Do they need to begin to look for a new leader?

Do you have a favourite, or a new favourite in the team you are leading? (N.B. That's always a dangerous thing - **_never_ have favourites in your team**).

Their future and their livelihoods depend on you. They depend upon your continued success, they depend on the state of your health, and your moods and how consistent you are also depend on your health.

If you think about it in these terms, they are perfectly right to examine and judge you, aren't they? Before ou became a leader didn't you do exactly the same thing? Of course you did.

And of course, you are judging them back at the same time. We can't help ourselves. And of course, your team are also judging each other, we are human.

Probably best bring your "A" game to work then. - Might be worth investing in a couple of bottles of vitamins, go back to the gym and eat better - just to be on the safe side…

Authority

Is a perfectly normal and pretty common word. Most of us use it a quite a lot and because of that we take its meaning for granted, don't we? We have all probably heard or read phrases like:

"By the authority invested in me..."

"By whose authority?..."

"He has the authority to..."

Or:

"You don't have the authority..."

They are all familiar enough phrases, aren't they?

In fact, they are so familiar that we tend not to give them much thought.

But we should.

As leaders and managers we need to give this word some thought and attention because, as leaders, authority is what we "do," so we have to be very concerned about the word. The reasons we are able to do what we do is because we have the authority. Besides, if we don't know where our right to tell people what to do comes from, what will we do if we are challenged?

If we don't have a good answer then team discipline might collapse and fall into a heap. If that happens it can take months and you, or your ex-bosses have to pay someone like me to put right. - And they really, really don't wat to do that.

So let's start with some kind of definition. This is from the Oxford Reference dictionary:

"Legitimate power, decision-making capacity, and the means to cause others to obey."

Let's dissect that for a moment.

"Legitimate power." It's a nice thought, isn't it? Noble, even. But is it only about legitimate power? What if someone is pointing a gun at you? They definitely have power over you but you can't say it is legitimate, can you? So shall we just say "power"?

"Decision-making capacity," a quite simple phrase to understand and a good thing: things have to be run by us and checked and agreed by us before they are acted upon. That seems to me to be to be a positive thing. After all, it's likely that we are the ones that will be paying for, or signing off, expenditures.

What about that "the means to cause others to obey" that could be a bit sinister, couldn't it? Of course, we are not the military or the police, so as far as we are concerned, I would say that the biggest sanction we have if everything goes badly wrong is to sack them.

So we can say that part of our authority come from our ability to sanction them in some way. A kind of "Do this, or else." In a softer manner, you might say

So we have our authority due to combination of:
1.   A measure of us having power,
2.   Our ability to make decisions
3.   The ability to get rid of those that don't do as we say or fit in.
4.   Daddy owns the company and daddy said you're in charge now.

It's not a bad set of reasons why we can have authority, is it? But, in fact, it reminds me of what Douglas MacGregor (the 1960s management guru, not the bloke on YouTube) would call a "Theory X" definition.

But, as we know, there is also "Theory Y," the more humane side of leadership and management.

* * *

What could some of the "Theory Y" reasons?

How about:

1.   **Prestige** - it's obvious that you know what you are talking about and you are good at doing it, so even though you have come out of left field you are now in charge and almost everyone is content about it.

2.   **You Were Elected** - there has been some kind of election, or competition and you won by popular acclaim. Or you were just chosen

3.   Last Chance: There's no-one else who can lead us because there is no-one else left who will do it.

In the end, it doesn't matter how you have been installed as a leader or manager because that will probably only get you through the first week or two anyway. It's how you do in every other week afterwards that counts.

BUT, in my experience, those that got the job by being a theory Y will have a much greater chance of lasting because those who they are leading will tend to accept them as a leader, rather than just acquiesce to them.

Mutinies do happen, even in civilian life, but before they do there's normally a long, long period of losing authority. It is hardly ever a gradual process. It starts slowly a bit like an avalanche, but then a moment comes when authority just evaporates as though it had never existed.

So how on earth do we maintain our authority? Well, as I have said elsewhere, by giving the people we lead

1.   a "vision" - a noble one sentence story of what we are doing and why.

2.   The knowledge that you are doing this for them and their best interests and not just yours.

* * *

3.		That you are giving them a sense of
	1. camaraderie,
	2. equity (by which I mean equality within the team) and that their work gives them a sense of
	3. achievement.

While we're here, yet again, I recommend you getting hold of a copy of Douglas MacGregor's book "The Human Side Of Enterprise" Although it may seem old now, It would be a good addition to your leadership and management library. It was first published in 1960, it will tell you all about theory X and theory Y management.

When I was a young trainee manager, it was required reading for anyone who had any ambitions to be a good manager.

The book speaks to us in a quaint tone and from a bygone era. The breathless anticipation he gives to the then upcoming eras of computerisation and Human Resources are kind of cute.

Respect

Obviously, we need to be respected in order to successfully lead a team. If you don't think so then just imagine yourself trying to lead a team where you are *not* respected. Sends shivers down the spine, doesn't it?

Great teams have respect for everyone but where does that come from and how do we get more?

There is a form of "Agile" management called Scrum, we use it I recommend it to you as something to find out more of. (In fact, I wrote a sister book to this one called "Going Agile").

One of the core values of Scrum is that there is a belief that everyone working in the team must treat each other with respect at all times.

Achieving this in some teams is a really hard and long slog. Please don't underestimate the amount of effort required in changing the working culture of an organisation that does not treat each other with respect.

If you want to find out more, skip to the "Ethics" section of this book whcih follows this section.

For now let's leave it as if you do this, and do it with sincerity, and you will have done all you need to do.

Best of luck!

ETHICS

Work Ethics

This is where we set the tone of how the team will engage with itself and with those outside such as stakeholders and clients.

Although this is one of the areas where you may feel uncomfortable in getting involved, and so not want to concentrate on at all, it is vital that you do get involved and do it right.

Let's be honest, most organisations only do this through their HR department - and you can guess how successful this can be. This is different - we are enforcing a set of ethics that apply to our team.

If you do enforce good work ethics and get it right you can make a huge difference to how you are perceived as a successful leader by your team and also teams around you. If you don't pay attention to this then it can lead to all sorts of bad behaviours by individuals in your team.

Be aware, if bad behaviour by individuals is tolerated at all by you, then the team will blame you more than those who actually behave badly. If it persists then you will be perceived as weak.

And a weak leader never lasts.

One of the most popular Agile management frameworks is called Scrum. They claim it has more than twelve million followers whcih makes it by far the most popular of the agile frameworks.

Scrum has what it calls "ways of working" and they are called the Scrum Values. These are the rules that it insists that people who follow Scrum use in working with each other.

We at Scrumnastics use these values and have them as our core ways of working. We actually use a few more too, but rather than list what they are I thought I would talk about these. The reason for this is that I think that the Scrum Values are much more likely to be followed by you and your team than some extra ones from some bloke who wrote a book.

* * *

For completeness, let's spend a little time on them now.

Scrum Values

Full disclosure, I hold the ethics promoted by the Scrum agile management framework to be really effective. They make for a calmer team, they make for a more productive team and they make for a team that produces better quality work.

There are five core Scrum values that the whole team (and the stakeholders) live by. These are:

Commitment, Focus, Openness, Respect, and Courage.

The official 2020 Scrum Guide™ uses the following words to describe how to implement them:

"The Scrum Team commits to achieving its goals and to supporting each other. Their primary focus is on the work of the Sprint to make the best possible progress toward these goals. The Scrum Team and its stakeholders are open about the work and the challenges. Scrum Team members respect each other to be capable, independent people, and are respected as such by the people with whom they work. The Scrum Team members have the courage to do the right thing, to work on tough problems.
These values give direction to the Scrum Team with regard to their work, actions, and behavior. The decisions that are made, the steps taken, and the way Scrum is used should reinforce these values, not diminish or undermine them. The Scrum Team members learn and explore the values as they work with the Scrum events and artifacts. When these values are embodied by the Scrum Team and the people they work with, the empirical Scrum pillars of transparency, inspection, and adaptation come to life building trust."

Lovely words, I'm sure you'll agree. However, if I went to a Managing Director or a potential client and told them that is how we were going to spend their money in order to get what they wanted done then I would probably get shown the door and told to shut it behind me.

Anyway, this is how we use the words:

Commitment: The team are committed to working full-time on your project and no other. They are committed to working in a collaborative manner with your team.

Focus: We commit to concentrate on delivering the one, agreed, Sprint goal to you.

Openness: We work in a completely transparent manner and all work is available for inspection at all times

Respect: As the client, you are part of the team. We want to work with you and with each other in an atmosphere of support and mutual respect for each other's talents, aptitudes and skills.

Courage: we will always deliver any 'bad news' early to you, so that together we can take appropriate steps to alter direction, minimise costs and mitigate risk.

Whichever version of the words you come with for yourself is entirely up to you, but you are welcome to use ours.

Why bother?

All these values may sound a little 'waffly' to you, but there is actually a hard-nosed reason you implement the Scrum Values: they improve the efficiency and productivity of the team and improve the quality of the work being delivered.

In Scrum, the Scrum Master (think team leader, team captain or foreman) is the person responsible for implementing the values, but the whole team and the stakeholders are responsible for making sure that everyone abides by them at all times.

The Scrum Values tend either to be the easiest part of Scrum to implement, or the very hardest. This will depend almost entirely upon your team's composition, your organisation's environment and your existing work culture.

Implementing and upholding commitment, focus, openness, respect and courage in a new, lean startup is a whole lot easier than doing it in a large, mature, traditional, bureaucratic, command-and-control organisation with a definite bias of 'us and them' from the management. After all, there are professional CEO's who can earn fabulous bonuses on the promise of changing a corporate culture. And most of them fail (though they still seem to get the bonuses).

Nevertheless, even if you are working in a toxic, bullying work culture, you *must* implement these good values inside your team from the very start. Why? Because the team sense that they are going to be treated fairly in the way that they work, and that makes a great deal of difference to the productivity of the team.

Whatever behaviours happen outside your (Scrum) team in the wider work environment must not interfere with the ethics and behaviours *inside* your team. Enforcing this can be a real challenge but then, being a Scrum Master/leader is *not* a job for the floppy or the faint-hearted.

Now I have been met with a rather scoffing attitude from a particularly hairy chested Managing Director about using the Scrum Values, I found that asking them the following helped enormously.

"Would[4] you rather this work be done with Commitment, Focus, Openness, Respect and Courage, or would you rather the work was done Without Commitment, Without Focus, Without Openness, Without Respect, or Without Courage?"

Being a leader (or Scrum Master) is not for the faint-hearted, is it?

---

[4] Stand up straight, draw yourself up to your full height, shoulders back, talk deep, low, and slowly. Do not blink and look them straight in the eye while saying:

86

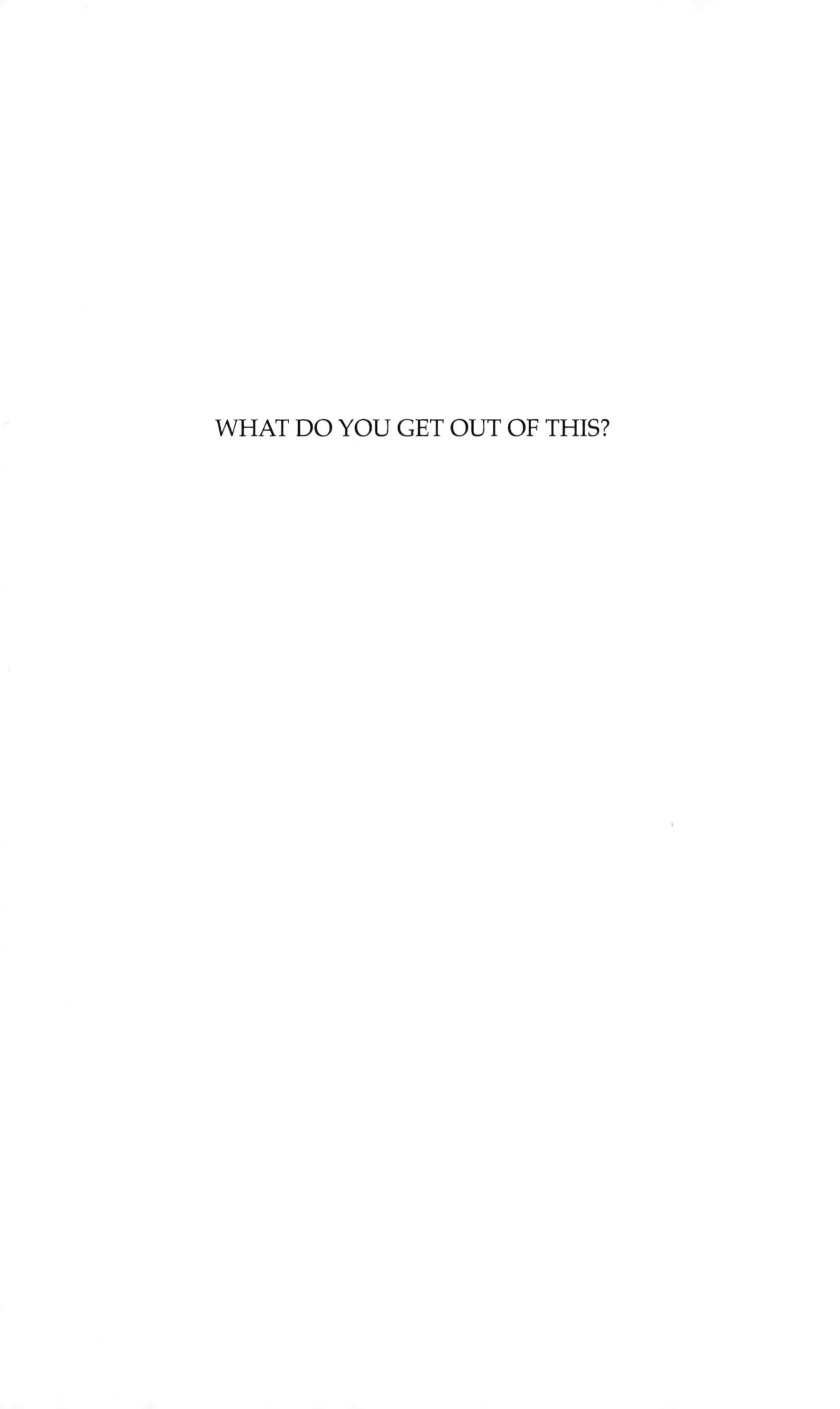

WHAT DO YOU GET OUT OF THIS?

What's the payback for you in being a good leader?

It's a fundamental question, isn't it? We have all seen examples of terrible leaders around us who thrive, don't they?

So why should we be any different?

One answer to it depends entirely on your personality and, whether or not you were brought up right.

If you do as I have been saying, what do you get out of all of this effort? After all, it seems that you won't be getting much back in comparison to the actions of your normal, British Standard, run-of-the-mill, technocratic sociopath , will you?

Where's the exhilaration of the power trip as you walk in? Where's the status harvesting that comes of making your minions feel small, and in comparison making your self big and inflating your ego?

I mean, what's in it for you? There doesn't seem to be much of a payoff for any self respecting, self regarding psychopathic bully to get their daily hit, does there?

And if you are one of these people, there isn't.

So why do it like this? Why go to all the bother?

Simple: you get to be a better person than you were. Also, a bigger person than you were. And you get to be trusted and respected. Truly respected, rather than fsimply eared by the people who are in your charge.

And for the right kind of person that is a worthwhile return.

To be sure, you will not be getting a loud, brash, instant rush of adrenaline every time you see your people scurry away from you in a rush to look busy. Rather, it is a quiet, calm as you bring and encourage an atmosphere of calm efficiency in which your people work quietly and efficiently.

Of course, for the wrong kind of person this will not not appeal at all. That's fine. Why? Because slowly but surely, the leader of the calm team will magnetically attract the very best of your team and so outperform and outcompete what's left of your team and leave you in the dust.

It's a litle bit similar to becoming a parent. Why do you put yourself through all the exhaustion, anguish and expense to do it? Well, in a similar way to becoming a leader, there are many reasons but one of the quiet reasons is that it makes you a better person.

But there is another reason. If you want your team to perform at their best they all need to be able to think clearly at all times. And that means calm.

Human beings can either think and act rationally, or they can be emotional. They can't do both at the same time.

In the teams that we lead, we need thinking people thinking clearly and all the time.

Think about how we are sold to. Advertisers try their hardest to attach some kind of emotion to their products and services so that we will buy it without thinking. Instead of thinking why we should buy something we will get a warm emotional feeling instead - and just buy the thing.

Think of social media and how it works on us. It works on us because the whole point of it is to elicit strong emotional responses from us. These strong emotional responses trigger fight or flight hormones in our bodies even when there is no real physical danger to us.

We can be emotional, or we can think.

As an example, when we do a project, we need the people we are managing people to think their best thoughts at all times, because that is how we get excellent work out of them.

In fact, we make it a condition that they put their phones away at the start of the working day and pick them up at lunchtime or at the end of the day. Why? Because we know from experience that highly emotionally charged workers do not work very well.

So what about the type of leader who thinks that scaring the pants of their team is good for productivity? They are wrong.

And that is why you want your team to work calmly and why you make every effort to keep them emotionally stable.

But Perhaps There Is Another Reason Why…

What if the received wisdom of how companies are run is coming to an end?

I know, mad, eh? After all, we live in a linear world where progress is progress, it is obviously unstoppable and we abandon what went before. So what do I know?

But if I told you that for twenty years was a data modeller who worked for a lot of global companies would you just bear with me?

We know the script, don't we? Two or three super clever undergraduates drop out before they graduate college with a brilliant idea, and three years later with some help from some venture capitalists they are all billionaires and world famous. Hooray.

But that is not the traditional way that companies were built. Traditionally, building a company was a slow, boring business that has often taken generations to build. Think of Japanese companies like Toyota and Panasonic. Vastly successful

So what? We do it differently now

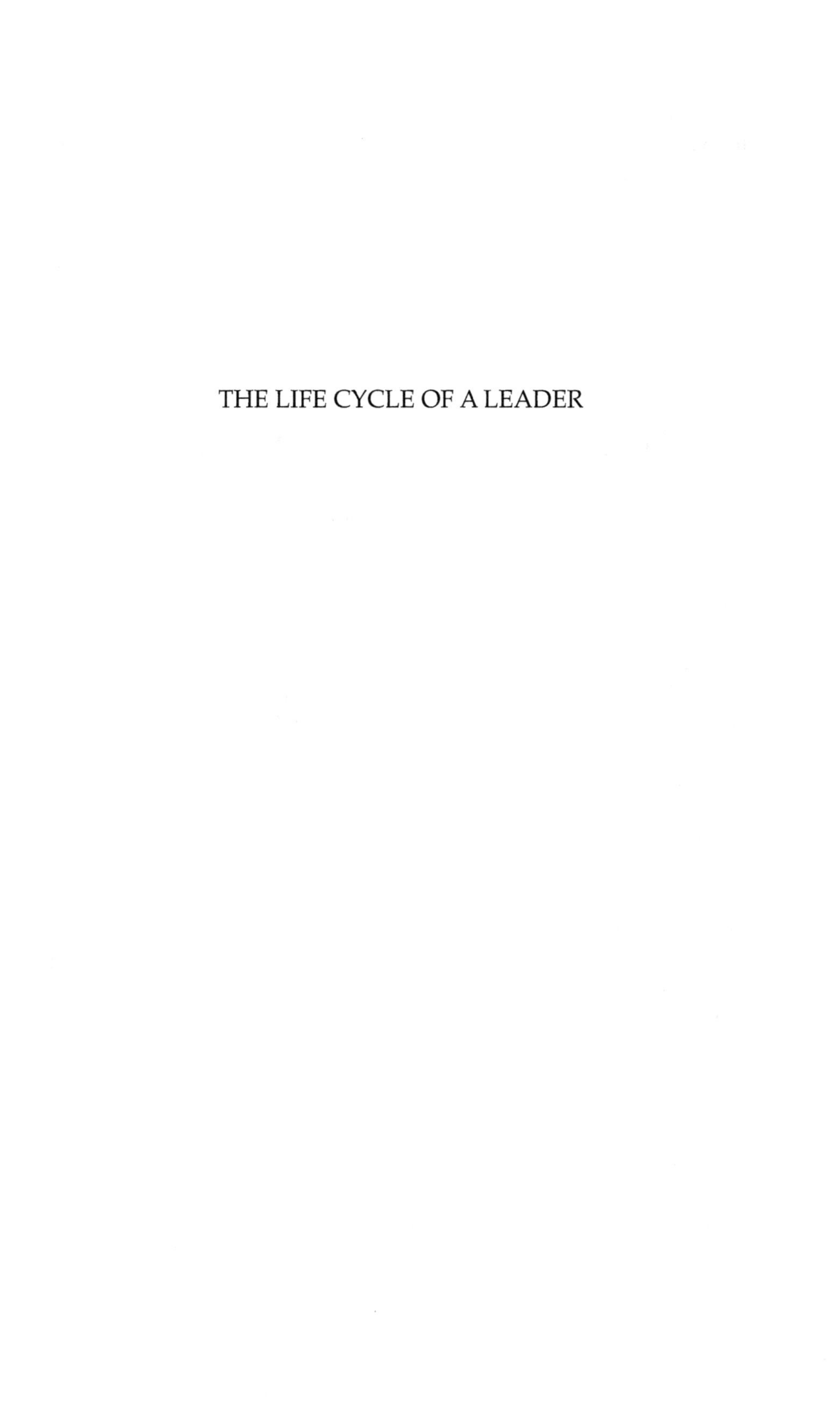

THE LIFE CYCLE OF A LEADER

Okay, that was a joke. If you think that all the leaders we have had for the past thirty years in politics, business, and the media are just fine and dandy, Amazon offer a 30 day money back guarantee on this book - I have nothing to offer you.

However, if you feel that their career report cards could be marked with a cursory "could do better," then please read on.

Why Do We Need A Constant Supply of New Leaders?

Because leaders have a shelf life. They come to an end.

They get bored, some get tired, some get ineffective and some just get old. You know, like human beings naturally do.

Then there's the situation where the world changes somehow and all their ideas and campaigns just no longer work because the environment has changed and they don't have the ability to change.

This situation is very dangerous to a company or organisation because most of the people around them or above them don't realise that the world has changed too and so they often respond by "doubling down" (doing a lot more of the same).

The only industry I have ever seen deal well with this is banking. The reason? Although bankers won't tell you this, they know that all finance companies eventually go bang. Therefore, they spend a great deal of their time looking for the next latest, greatest small to medium finance company, buy it and look over every month's figures like a hawk.

They even have teams of senior managers whose only focus is to slash and burn and cut all costs.

At the very first hint of the numbers not being quite so magic they sack the executives and put their own special types in to shut it down before too much money is lost. Then on they go again, onto the next one. I didn't say it was pleasant, it's just how the are.

Anyway, that's management, let's get back to leaders.

There's an old cliche,isn't there, that says, "everyone loves a winner." And it is true: In just about everything we do, people find success attractive.

And failure? It is the opposite - we find it desperately unattractive.

When a new leader is installed (or emerges), there is an energy, an optimism and vigour that surrounds them to begin with. They just can't seem to do any wrong whatsoever. It's all very attractive.

Call it knowledge, call it expertise, call it a mysterious combination of things but, inevitably, there is a part of it which is pure luck.

And, one day unfortunately, luck runs out.

To err is human, isn't it? Leaders must make mistakes if they are human. It is inevitable: some will be small, some will be larger, and unfortunately, there's that catastrophic one.

But this enthusiasm for the new boss doesn't last forever. After either a long or a short time, the gloss of their ideas and personality wear a bit thin and the mistakes pile up and get remembered.

And then one day it is all over bar the wailing and gnashing of teeth and the cries of "my staff have let me down!"

For human beings, when they get rid of a leader it is just their reputation that is shredded on their way out the door. But our nearest mammal relative, chimpanzees, things really, really don't end well at all. And it's often worse if you are a lion. Let's just say it's good to be human.

Anyway, the point is that a leader can't and won't last forever. There is a life cycle, and it ends.

* * *

There are two points here:

1.   If leaders have a limited life you'd better have another leader close at hand who is ready to take over, hadn't you?

2. If you have a purely top down leadership model then the transition from the old to the new can be rocky, especially during the transition period where the old guard of the next level down are being replaced.

Of course, the idea we need to keep at the back of our mind is that it might just be you getting the old heave-ho.

And it might be nice to have someone you actually know to hold the door open for you on your way out...

SOME CONCEPTS

I said earlier that leadership is a craft, so what sort of "tools" do we have, then?

Every trade needs its special tools like special saws, hammers, screwdrivers and spanners that are preculiar to it. What do we have?

Well, we have some concepts about how human beings behave when they are in groups, and that is what we are going to look at now.

Always remember when you are leading that you always have two choices:

1.	To let the people in your organisation work in a way that reflects how they seem to work naturally and take advantage of the benefits that arise.

2.	To force your people to work in a way that bureaucracy demands

The "Span of Control"

Not too difficult to grasp, the span of control is simply is the number of people that report up to another person, (or are controlled by someone, depending on your point of view).

Now, your job as a leader is to get your ideas into the heads of as many people as you need to , as quickly as you can, and as effectively and efficiently as you can.

That means that the ratio has to be more than one, doesn't it? Which brings us to our first issue: there are many organisations, especially in the public sector, where the ratio is just 1:1. The first question you and I would proably have in that situation is, "how much genuine leadership is going on here?"

These are the people who will tell you this is fine because they are technocrats. I am really not a fan of technocracy, especially of its one hundred year history, so I would not agree with that assessment.

I think that is a question we should leave to them to answer but we have established something: based on what has been said above, a ratio of 1:1 is probably not an efficient environment for effective leadership.

So if that is a poor leadership environment, what does a good one look like?

Of course, there has to be balance. If you have too many reporting to you then the potential for misunderstanding and mistakes becomes very big. On the other hand, if you have too few then your organisation or company is not making the most efficient use of your time.

The Goldilocks question:

How many is too many, how many is too few, and what seems to be "just right."?

Well, we could spend a fortune trying to find out or we could just take the advice of those who have gone before and done the work for us

After the carnage of the First World War, the British army wanted to investigate if it could organise itself better in the future to avoid so much carnage.

General Sir Ian Hamilton was asked to go and find out if there was a way. In 1922 he published a report called "The Soul And Body Of An Army," with his findings .

This is what he wrote

"The nearer we approach the supreme head of the whole organization, the more we ought to work towards groups of three; the closer we get to the foot of the whole organization, the more we work towards groups of six." - General Sir Ian Hamilton, "The Soul And Body Of An Army," 1922

So, he thought between one to three and one to six, depending on how senior the ranks you are delaing with.

Of course, we are taking about armies which have to act and be successful in situations where bullets are flying. That probably isn't us, so is it useful for us?

Well, this kind of ratio crops up time and again in all sorts of situations.

Let's look at the scouts. Obviously, there is no shooting involved but they are organising young, inexperienced, probably very excitable boys and girls. Potentially, this is a recipe for complete bedlam, - what do they do? Traditionally, scouts are organised into teams of six, and their leader is called a "sixer." It works for them.

* * *

Scrum, which is one of the most popular "agile" management frameworks, recommends the ideal size of a self managing team is six people.

So, what do we know? Well, we can see that there are real organisations runnning real groups of practical people who have hit upon a set of numbers that seem to work in the real world. I might be an idea ot follow their example?

I would say that we have the answer to the Goldilocks question. Between 3 and 6 is the optimum.

Yes but…

Okay, Nick, I have fifteen people who answer to me. What do I do?

Although three to six seem to be the optimum, you can certainly go larger without having to write a long, bureaucratic procedures manual.

Have you ever wondered why most sports teams have eleven people in them?

Football? Eleven. Cricket eleven.

Why is that? Why not twelve? Or thirteen?

Is it to do with the fact that the whole point of a sports team is to win and about eleven is the maximum size of team you can put together before it all descends into chaos? Well it could be.

And of course, the smart bloke at the back of the room is thinking, "Yeah, but what about rugby union teams? They have fifteen!"
They do, don't they?

But the thing about a rugby team is that it is split into two sub teams: the forwards and the backs.

* * *

Which do completely different jobs. So different that it is like having two different teams, one of eight people and one of seven on the field at the same time.

Why am I wittering on about this? Because whenever I have had more than eleven but less than sixteen in a team I simply split them up into two teams - and it works very well.

Okay, but I have forty five people…

A bit more problematic, but not at all unmanageable.

The largest project I have ever managed had 168 people on it and was in a very sorry state when I took it over. How did I manage to turn it round? I split the people on the project into a load of separate teams, each made up of between six and eleven people each.

Now that's a lot of teams, so how did I get them to co-ordinate with one another?

I stole an idea from the book of Exodus, in the Old Testament.

When Moses took the Israelites out of Egypt he became their judge over disputes. After a short time things got heated and he was accused to being a tyrant.

So his father in law (who wasn't Jewish) told him to put the Israelites into groups of ten, and the tenth person was to be an elder. The elder judged simple disputes.
If the dispute was more serious, then it was raised to a higher group made up of ten elders of the ten groups of ten who judged that.

Then if it was more serious, the most senior elder and nine of his peers from that level…

You get the idea.

We simply made sure that every one of the teams had position called a Product Owner (it is a role in Scrum) and each Product Owner became a member of the next level up. And, of course, the chief Product Owners became members of the next level up again.

And it works. I have used it many times since and it always works.

I won't bore you with the ins and outs, but it shows just how you could do the same without having to build a huge, clunky set of procedures and a whole set of rulebooks to get stuff done.

So this is an example of where a simple, bottom up method of leadership and management can be quickly scaled up to accomodate quite large teams with a really quite flat management structure.

Remember that the whole point of of a flat management structure is to save money on administration so that you can spend more on the truly productive workers.

And that gives you a competitive advantage.

You Don't Always Need Big Groups To Do Big Things.

Have you ever seen a picture of a Lamborghini Miura? It was developed in the mid 1960s and to this day, it still looks like its doing one hundred miles an hour even when it is parked, and is featured in the 1960's classic film "The Italian Job."

Small teams can achieve amazing things. For example, the prototype of this beautiful car, the Lamborghini Miura, was made in 1967 - By a team of seven people

The seven people in the team made it in six months. *After work*. In their spare time.

Figure 1 The Lamborghini Miura[5] from 1967 - Built by seven people - Vroom…

Ferruccio Lamborghini, the boss of the company didn't even get to see the finished prototype until he saw it at the Motor Show on the Lamborghini stand.

And the designer, Marcello Gandini, was 22. I know. All that talent.

---

[5] Photograph kindly supplied by bernswaelz, (and paid for by me).

Sickening, isn't it?

For some people (okay, me), this is the most beautiful car ever made. It is an exquisite example of 20th century kinetic industrial art, because it looks as though it is doing a million miles an hour even when stood still. It makes men of a certain age murmur "Vroom…" quietly, under their breath.

But the key point is that it was made by a small team of seven people, each with their own, specific skills. Not seventy. Not seven hundred. Seven. What can a small team accomplish? The Lamborghini Miura, that's what.

Small teams can do amazing things.

Now in certain branches of what they call management but we might not, having huge numbers of people in your organisation under you is a real badge of importance. Technocrats and bureaucrats just love to boast how many people they are responible for.

But are they really personally responsible for them? I once interviewed a man who was the UK manager of a facilities management company who claimed he was responsible for more than 4,350 people in the UK. When I asked him how many people reported directly to him he said seven.

Seven people reported to him directly, not 4,350.

But apart from the status harvesting of pretending that people manage thousands of people directly, why on earth should we even want to pretend?

Let's talk about Thomas Ringelmann and Derek De Solla Price

Max Ringelmann and Price's Law

Max Ringlemann

Max Ringelmann experimented more than a hundred years ago on how much the work rate diminishes as you add people to a group. He studied a tug-o-war team and measured how hard each individual could pull when pulling on their own. Then he put all eight members onto the rope and measured how hard they pulled when all together. The result? He found when they pulled together, they only gave 50% of the total amount of potential power.

What did he learn that is valuable to us? He learned that putting a group of individuals in the same room and calling them a team doesn't actually do an awful lot. You need to do some extra things to make them work better, and that's why so many people did so much work on designing ways to make teams work better.

Derek John de Solla Price's "Price's Law: (the 'power law')

Even more demoralising, there's even a 'law' of reducing work called "Price's Law," (by Derek John De Solla Price). Price's Law states that 50% of all work in an environment is done by the square root of the number of people involved.

That's a posh way of saying most of the work gets done by very few people. Worse, adding lots of people just makes it worse.

So if we have the following employee numbers:

Number of Employees	50% of Work done by…
10	3
50	7
100	10

| 500 | 22 |
| 1000 | 31 1/2 |

Just a quick glance at the table above tells you why the' big guy' businesses want to be like the 'small guy' businesses.

Personally, lookimg at this table I am just relieved I don't have to justify the salaries of the 1,000 employee business to any hot-shot stock exchange analysts doing a revenue-per-employee examination for the shareholders, especially if the shareholders have heard of De Solla Price..

In fact, many of the companies that I admire most (like Toyota and Honda) do most of their future development using small teams. In other words, they pretend to be small companies.

But Who Are These 50% People?

There are some people who are just better than others. It is totally unfair but it just is.

In programming, data sciences and project management we call these people the "10X people."

They normally cost twice as much as your regular 'resource,' so most project managers won't touch them - but they are missing their whole point.

10X people may cost twice as much but they are normally ten times as productive. Not only that but their enthusiasm is incredibly infectious to the rest of the team so much so that it rubs off to the the rest of them. Everyone in the team is lifted up, their enthusiasm for the work raises and everyone's pace quickens.

Oh, did I mention that they are SO easy to manage? In fact, as a leader and a manager you have to work hard to keep their workloads up because they work so fast (and to an incredibly high standard, too) .

* * *

So if you are ever charged with initiating a project and you are looking through a bunch of CVs and notice a couple of 'rock stars' there, do not be put off by the day rate - there is a good reason they can command that money.

So What Did We Just Learn?

Span Of Control

We talked about the span of control and what it is.

WE know that if you have a large and complex organisation then the ratio of boss to employee shold be 1:3 and as you move down to the lower ranks it is okay to increase that ratio to 1:6.

Note that you don't have to increase the ratio. In infantry units ae around the 1:6 range but most special forces act in groups of three.

 We are also clued up enough now to make sure our 'spidey-sense' is triggered if we are in an environment where the ratio of boss to employee is 1:1 (you will see this a lot in NHS trusts, for example).

Small teams can achieve massive things

We briefly looked at the example of how an exquisite piece of 1960s Italian automotive history was made by seven people (really five) who did it in the spare time.

Small teams can not only achieve massive success but small teams move more rapidly than large teams too.

Ringelmman and De Jolla Price

Ringelmann

We looked at Max Ringelmann and his tug of war examinations before the first world war and we saw that he found team players were only giving 50% of their potential when they were in a team of eight.

There are techniques to boost this significantly, and I wrote two books called "Goiing Agile," and "Scrumnastics"which talk about these (or you could go to scrum.org and read all about it there

But it also illustrates the old saying "If you want to go fast, go alone. If you want to go far, go in a group."

De Jolla Price

We talked briefly about De Jolla Price's 'power law' where 50% of the work in any organisation is done by the square root of the number of employees.

What did we find? Well, if it is true that 50% of the work

LEADERSHIP TECHNIQUES

The Vision

The "Vision" that you have to come up with is basically a very short story. A short story of how you intend to get to where you say you want to go and take your people. It can be done in words (but not too many, two sentences ought to do it), or a picture (even better, because, as the old cliche goes, a picture is worth a thousand words) , or best of all, a picture and a sentence or two.

It may sound a bit daft, or even infantile at first. Draw a picture? Write a couple of sentences? However, doen well, it the one of most powerful tools in the toolbox of the leader. Do this bit right and people will follow you to the ends of the earth. Do it badly and they will drift away from you at the drop of a hat.

But first, a question for all of us: Why on earth should a bunch of sensible, highly skilled and experienced adults, many of who have existing responsibilities to their familes and loved ones allow to to you to lead them?

In short, why should they follow you?

The answer? Naked self interest on their part and trust in you. Despite what the HR department foolishly hopes, they are not there simply because of you being you and them wanting to bathe in the reflected glory of your magnificence.

As well as the money you are paying them (which is taken as read), people are always in search of an extra something, or some things that are beside just making them better off or keep the wolf from the door. For another week As we know from elsewhere in this book, those three things are:

1.   A sense of achievement in their work.

2.   That they are treated with equity (no, I don't mean DEI, I mean a sense of fairness within the team (no favourites).

3. A spirit of camaraderie, or 'esprit de corps,' (spirit of the body) at

work

4. All of which will raise their status in their eyes, and the eyes of others

How do you give them that? Well, a good start is to give them a great reason, or bunch of reasons, to follow you.

This can give them a great reason WHY they should follow you instead of all the other options that they have in front of them.

They know that the future is coming for all of us. It won't be long until it is Christmas, then spring, and then summer.

What you have to convince them of is that when next Christmas, spring and summer come, THEY will be better off than if they hadn't followed you, and they will have spent their time in doing something more worthwhile than if they hadn't been with you.

In order to do that you need to give them a great vision of what you want to achieve and to share that vision of where you are going with them - and where you will expect to arrive.

It can just be a one or two sentence word picture of where you intend to go, a picture (a cartoon, even) or a combination (my favourite).

Of course, this requires that you spend some time actually thinking about where you want to go and how to go about it - and this is harder than it sounds and takes longer than you think. And to be prepared to modify that vision as you go towards achieving it.

But just by doing this you will be better than at least two thirds of the leaders that are around you in Britain today. For as we know, we are being let down by what journalists call a "managerial class."

And the biggest problem with the managerial class is that they often can't actually manage anything.

Do my job for a bit and you will realise that there are a lot of leader/

managers who want the job, the salary and, most of all the status, but they don't want to do the work required in order to even barely scrape by doing the job, never mind be interested in getting really good at it. In other words they just want the 'trappings' of being a leader but not the hard work.

But not you , best beloved leadernomist, not you.

You are going to spend time on your own doing some old fashioned thinking and imagining and some dreaming. Because you have to. You have to come up with a vision that persuades and inspires others to want to get involved and bring it, kicking and screaming, and often reluctantly, into reality.

Even better, once you have shared your initial vision with them you will have the confidence to release it to them and allow your vision to be modified and shaped by them in order to make it an even better vision. You wil allow them to 'buy-in' to your vision and so make it better.

As Nietsche said, *"Man can endure many hows with a strong enough why."*

Which is just a posh way of saying that with a good strong vision your people won't leave you in the lurch, which is always when you need them most.

Now, coming up with a vision statement can be hard, especially if you have never done one, or you don't even know anyone who has ever done one. So here are two sets of words I always use to come up with a vision statement. Feel free to copy them for your own purposes.

From a mildly negative standpoint:

"To subvert the (large thing/major players/) by making the best (thing/service) available to normal people that was until now, only available to the wealthiest people in the land."

* * *

I wish I could say that I came up with this but I didn't. It was created by Peter Drucker, the twentieth century management guru and economist of the Austrian school. Anyway, if it is good enough for him to use, it will surely be fine for us.

I never fail to be delighted by the glee that comes over the faces of the most strait laced managers when we do a seminar and I make them use the opening phrase "To subvert the…"

From a positive starting point:

"To build the very best (product/service) ever seen in our market and to improve people's lives at a price that (poor/ordinary/ moderately weatlhy/filthy rich) people can afford to make the world a better place."

These are just starting points for you but I and my colleagues find they are great to start the imagination working.

What do I mean by allowing your team to shape and change your initial plan?

Let's consider that you want to build a beautiful house. You have spent hours and days imagining what it will look like, how you will feel in it, what it will say to the world about you. You even have exquisite, cloth-of-gold plans of pure, breathtaking beauty drawn up by a hot-shot architect.

All you need is for some skilled, talented, burly builders go go ahead and build it for you.

But have you thought about the boring things like the foundations being suitable for the site? Do you have the knowledge to ven begin to hazard an educated guess? How about local planning restrictions? Those super snazzy house bricks - are they actually available in your area or will the planners even allow them? More to the point, do you have enough knowledge to that you CAN think about these things in an intelligent way?

* * *

You see, and I can tell you this as a project manager, in the world that we live in, there are people who charge a fortune for doing airey-fairy, lah-di-dah conceptual stuff, and there are those that actually do practical stuff like build houses, mend your car, do the plumbing and all the other things that stop silly people with more money than sense getting injusred in their own homes or dying horribly.

And you need to listen to them. Because they can save you money, heartache, misery and even your life and limbs.

What do they get out of helping you modify your vision of where you are going and want to achieve? Why, the satisfaction that their intervention probably saved the project from imminent disaster and also the very important ingredients for a great set of stories to tell their friends and drinking buddies next time they see them. (And you should never underestimate the value of your people having a few more 'war hero' stories to exchange with their colleagues).

The Voice Of Leadership

The 'voice of command' is a real thing - It is the manner in which you speak with your team in order to instill calm in them, it shows that you have an expectation that you will lead them, you know how to lead them and that allows them to have more confidence in you as their leader, which is always especially helpful in the beginning.

It is the voice of of someone who is speaking in a relaxed, unhurried way. The voice of command never competes with anyone. It has no need to: the voice's owner is in charge.

People speaking over you? Become silent. Silence is powerful. The person who has the confidence to be silent is the opposite of the chatterbox, or someone who has to compete. We do not compete. We are in charge.

Please do not confuse the voice of leadership with that put on, silly, braying, English public schoolboy, fake deep voice that you will hear fro someone trying too hard to convince you that they have the stuff of leadership in every fibre of their being. That is fake. Everyone listening to it also knows it is fake and it convinces or fools no-one.

If you do use that way of talking at the right now, please know that everyone you talk to knows what you are trying to do. It is that obvious. Worse, they ALL know that it is fake, and, unfortunately, that is how you will appear. Besides, the next time you speak with someone who has a naturally deeper and more relaxed voice than you, you will _shrivel_ inside and your team will probably see it too - not good at all.

All you have to do to use the voice of leadership is to relax your voice so that you naturally talk as deeply as is natural for you. Speak quietly, and slowly. This will help them listen to you and also help you keep your nerve, whch will stop your voice from breaking into a squeak. Squeaks are not good.

The low voice also demonstrates how much testosterone you were exposed to when you were an adolescent (this works for women as well, notice how many women senior managers have low voices). The lower the voice, the more testosterone you made when it was important. The more testosterone you have been exposed to, the greater the potential aggression you can potentially harness and summon, and the more potential harm you can do to someone else. As the saying goes, it's not the dog in the fight, it's the fight in the dog.

There's something else about speaking in the most naturally low voice. Apparently, the neurons in your brain that receive and decode speech themselves vibrate and resonate with lower frequancies and they don't with higher frequencies.

So how do you naturally get to speak in as naturally low voice as you can muster? Practice.

Here's an old trick I learned from being a radio producer and presenter and doing radio programmes from deades ago. - And this really helps: You have to practice. Practice speaking deeply and slowly - it will allow your mouth to work slower than your brain. Making your mouth work slower than your brain is _really_ important when speaking in public.

In a radio studio, what you really don't want is for your mouth to be going faster than your brain. If you do, then you get awkward, silent, sound gaps, or 'air,' in the speech. Trust me, that _really_ freaks out your audience, because it creates a great big doubt in their mind that you know what you are saying and doing.

Similarly, when you are leading your team what you really don't want is your mouth working faster than your brain. Big gaps in speech make you look like a lemon. Look at politicians…

Strengthening your voice

Who has one of the greatest speaking voices in the world? For my money it has to be the actor Morgan Freeman. His voice is great isn't it? I could listen to him all day, even if he was reading out something as boring as the football results.

Did Morgan Freeman's voice just appear as an out-of-the-box

phenomenon? Well, although you might think it could, _he_ doesn't claim it was. He claims that his voice was the result of years of elocution and voice training. Of course, we don't have years to wait around but...

Morgan Freeman says the strongest factor of him getting that voice was due to one exercise: deliberate and repeated yawning.

Yes, that's right, yawning. I would say that if that technique is good enough for Morgan Freeman, then it's good enough for us.

So here is the exercise:

1.   Take yourself off to a quiet place where no-one can hear you.

2.   I want you to say "Hello, my name is (your name), and I am your new team leader/boss/manager."

3.   Give yourself a mark out of ten for each of the following:
            How tight your throat felt
            How relaxed you sounded
            How high your voice sounded
            How was the tone? Tinny? Rich?
            How quickly you spoke

4.   Take a deep breath in and out and force yourself to yawn three times. Really go to town on it. Now do it again. And again.

5.   Now repeat the phrase Hello, my name is (your name), and I am your new ..."

6.   Again, now give yourself a mark out of ten for each of the following:
            How tight your throat felt this time
            How relaxed you sounded this time
            How high your voice sounded this time
            How was the tone? Tinnier? Richer?
            How quickly you spoke this time

7.   Now try and reapeat this every day for seven days and

see if your scores improve

8. I need you to become mindful of how your voice changes during your work day and other social situations. What happens when:

You talk to your boss (it will probably tend to go higher, so try to keep it low)
You talk with different members of your family
You talk with your team
You talk in an unexpected situation (listen to how your changes under stress).

It is well worth pursuing and those that do are nearly always amazed when they begin to see their status increase in quite a short space of time.

I suppose the best recommendation I can give is that when I used to have a radio show, I always took myself off to the toilet five minutes before going on air and yawn ten times and I still do this before I speak in public.

It works for me, I hope it works for you.

Presence - Looking the Part

Turns Out Your Grandparents Were Right After All - Put You Shoulders Back, Stand Up Straight And Remember Those Lobsters[6]

A great deal of successful leadership is knowing how to lead – but an important part is possessing the *physicality* of leadership.

Why? Because your people are looking at you. Today. Tomorrow. Next week. And they are judging you.

What are they judging? Your physical strength. They are judging whether you are still capable of leading them today (yesterday is _over)_, and whether you are still worth following. They will do this every day. You think that heroic thing you did for the team last week will count for something next month? It won't.

We need to have and display that certain status that all leaders have. That certain weight, or heft, or if you are French, 'avoirdupois[7]'.

What grants someone that 'weight,' that'heft'? That certain something that gives them status? How did they get it?

More importantly, how do you get it?

In a word, your posture. How do you get an imposing, upright posture?Serotonin.

Serotonin is the universal status marker. Serotonin is the hormone that dictates how much status that we, chimps, lions, dogs and even lobsters have within the group we are in.

---

[6] If you don't believe any of this, go and read the first chapter in "12 Rules For Life: An Antidote To Chaos," by Jordan Peterson.

[7] French for 'Feel the weight.' Who'd want to use the phrase feel the weight when you can use avoirdupois?

* * *

The more serotonin in your bloodstream, the higher your status. Er, and that's about it. I wish it were more complicated than that, but unfortunately, it isn't. It is a 350-million-year-old system that is even older than the design of your lungs. And your skin, too.

You know that (yes, I know it is terribly immature) thing where you blast off from the traffic lights and burn off the guy in their rubbish car?

Why did you do that? You did it because you got a sudden rush of serotonin as a result, which raised your status.

Did you get a promotion, or a raise in salary at work? How is this raising of your status displayed to others? You get more serotonin, so your posture improves.

Get the brush off from that very attractive person who you know is out of your league but, hey, it's been a great day and God loves a try-er, so why not?

Less serotonin. Actually, quite a lot less serotonin. And rounded shoulders.

More than that, your brain (and everyone else's, too) has a really old, and incredibly clever little bit in it that knows _exactly_ how much serotonin you have.

Not only that, it compares the amount of serotonin _you_ have in your bloodstream, with the amount that everyone else has, while _their_ brains are doing the same thing for them at the same time. One of the ways it does this is examining your posture and comparing it with everyone else's.

It's how we all know our rank in life. And ranks change. We can go up and we can go down. In seconds.

Try it for yourself, the next time something positive happens to you, just pay attention to how your posture improves. Next time something negative happens, again, pay attention to how you slouch.

* * *

Also, be particularly aware of the actions of 'status vampires,' those creepy types who get their jollies by making themselves feel good at the expense of making other people feel bad. Britain is full of them. Why do they do it? For a quick hit of serotonin. It's nothing professional, it's entirely personal.

What is the easiest way for you to get more serotonin? Well, it is part of what is called a 'feedback loop.' The secret? Your posture. The better your posture, the more serotonin you make. Even better, the more serotonin you make the better your posture. It is what is known as a virtuous feedback circle.

So, your granddad and grandmother were right: Stand up straight, get your shoulders back (so your shoulder blades are touching), then suck your shoulders down into their sockets[8]. Look everyone straight in the eye and talk deeply and slowly. Practice that. In front of a mirror if you must, but practice.

Exercise 1:

No matter what your height, I want you to pull yourself up to your very tallest, pull your shoulders back and then go outside. Remember: shoulders back, chest out, chin tucked in. We are looking for an assertive posture here. There is absolutely no need to try to look aggressive or act in an aggressive manner while you are doing this.

In fact, try putting just a hint of a smile on your face. Now, walk down your road and as you pass by a stranger, maintain your most upright posture, stare impassively straight ahead and don't make direct eye contact.

This is the point: I want you to notice out of the corner of your eye what happens about five to seven metres before they pass by you.

* * *

---

[8] I know it sounds weird but the moment you do it right, you will suddenly feel stronger than you _ever_ have before. Go and ask Pavel Tsatsouline about it. He's right.

If you do it right, keeping your shoulders back and your head upright, you will notice that as they approach you, they will nod their head slightly. Almost imperceptibly, they bow.

What this means is that they have acknowledged you as having higher status, even though they don't know who you are. A complete stranger. Serotonin. It's a weird thing. But it works.

What's the point of this in relation to leadership? Well, like it or not we humans exist in tribal hierarchies, even in work. Let it work for you. As Battery Sergeant Major Williams used to say in the BBC comedy, "It Ain't Half Hot, Mum,"

"Fine pair of shoulders you've got there, show 'em off."

Exercise 2:

I want you to become mindful and aware of your own posture throughout the day and I want you to become aware how it changes as you interact with different people.

When you talk with this person, are you able to maintain a tall and erect posture, or do you feel your shoulders start to pull forward, and your back to slouch? Why do you think this is?

If your shoulders do droop, just try and quietly reset your posture to be as upright as you can. Try and notice what happens to the tone and direction of the conversation when you catch yourself pulling your shoulders back and putting your shoulder blades together. Remember to make yourself as tall as you can. Again, does the tone and the direction of the conversation change?

I urge my students to get into the habit of getting used to using this in as many different social situations as they can. It is a useful tool for gaining and honing knowledge about yourself as you interact with others.

* * *

Strength And Fitness:

Part of looking the part of a leader is how strong and fit you appear. Strength and vitality _matter_ in leadership. Look how many managers do sporty activities. You won't need to be the strongest in your team, but you do need to look robust.

After all, you will be required to champion your team at some point., probably against someone in your organisation. Your team need to know and have confidence that you have the wherewithal to defend them when it comes to it.

Many would say it is not my job to tell you to exercise and to watch what you eat, but I am going to anyway. The better you eat the stronger you will be. The physically stronger you are the better leader you will be, especially at the end of the working day. Leaders also need their cognitive (brain) strength and there is a link between fitness and cognitive strength. Leaders need to make good decisions at all times of the day. Your team need you to be strong because you are their champion.

Do like your mother told you: eat properly and stop eating processed food and get enough sleep. When you do start to eat well, you will soon feel fitter and stronger. Even better, make your own food and take it into work with you, especially at lunchtime. It will be better than the rubbish you buy from any sandwich shop. Watch the drinking, especially when on your own or at home.

Get fresh air. Every day. Get out at lunchtime and walk for twenty minutes. When you finish work get out and walk for another twenty minutes. Doing those two will make a huge difference to your fitness and your mental wellbeing. Leadership is strenuous so you need to nurture your body and form that your mind.

Our bodies were shaped by millions of years of activity. We were not designed for office work. Exercise, especially weights for muscle strength. You don't need a gym membership.

Do I do this? Yes. I am a keto carnivore, I use a rebounder every day, I do kettlebells and love being outside - but that's just me. I have no idea if the same thing will work for you, but I really think that investing some time and effort in finding some way of eating that works for you is important. Whatever it will eventually be, it's probably safe to say that kebabs, turkey twizzlers, chips, rice, white bread and biscuits are probably not doing you a great deal of good.

For me, kettlebells have offered a fantastic route to strength and fitness, but they are basically cannon balls with handles, so if you find the idea appealing you <u>*must*</u> learn how to use them properly.

The potential for particularly nasty injury is ever present with kettlebells. The best kettlebell person in the world is Pavel Tsatsouline, he has very good books and online courses and, for a Russian, also has a sense of humour, too.

Posture - Part Two - "Nerd Neck" and the "C" shaped person

When I was a young programmer, before they let you have a desk top computer, you had to pass a Health and Safety test where you were examined on whether you knew about how to sit safely at a computer (I am being serious). They also gave you a posture test before they let you on a computer.

Then along came laptops and all that went out of the window. Good posture? Who cares?

Then portable phones stopped being boring and became smart and all the really psychopathic psychologists came off the dole and went to earn big, big bucks manipulating people's minds through exciting their emotions. These days? Most people appear in the street to be under remote control by them - including our teams.

Did you know that as well as treating people for phoe addction, doctors have come up with two new medical conditions: "Nerd Neck," and "C" shaped people. These are physical conditions that didn't exist even twenty years ago, and arise out of the postures that people have evolved in order to use these things.

Now you may regard this as a first world problem but the fact is that if you are curved over into a "C" shape then it affects the amount of air you breathe in and out with every breath - not good at all.

The result is   poor posture which has a terrible effect on phyiscal and mental health.

We actually get our people to sign up to a no phone agreement where outside of tea breaks and lunchtimes, people do not use their phones because they are at work, damn it - and they find it really hard to do for the first few days.

We also insist that they go out for twenty minutes at lunchtime and five minutes at tea and coffee break just to see the sky, rain or shine. It is not pure altruism, we find that people just work better if they do.

Mind Your Language

I really mean it, mind your language. When you want something to happen give clear, direct, crisp instructions using clear, direct, crisp language in an active voice. Say "I want you to…" and not floppy millennial language. "I think it would be a good idea if you…" is pure floppy millennial language and not good enough. - You get the idea.

A lot of new leaders think that being direct is rude, but it isn't. In this day and age, it is actually quite a relief for someone to receive a direct request to do something. The more words you use for a request, the more it can be misinterpreted by the person listening. Do them a favour and get used to using short, crisp instructions that start with "I want you to…"

And don't swear - you are no longer "one of the boys" or "one of the girls." People you lead do not respect you using bad or intemperate language at any time. You are a leader; they expect better of you and frankly, they have a right to expect better of you.

One final thing: "Oi! You there at the back? Stand up straight when I'm talking to you!"

Ancient Archetypes Of Heroes And Why They Might Be Helpful To Us.

This is the part of the book where I expect you to be thinking, "What is he talking about now? Has he taken leave of his senses?"

But there is a point to it, I promise. What is the point? Well, during the last decade of the twentieth century, in the 1990s, a new phenomena arose: that of the "new man." They were incredibly successful. They were everywhere, especially in the corporate, media, arts and political worlds. You could spot them in their good suits, open necked shirts, MBAs and complete lack of ties.

These were a real stereotype: the "managerialists." They combined both being relaxed in their attitudes to making money and very liberal in their political views at the same time. Politically correct millionaires. In fact, although they thought of themselves as brand spanking new, they were not much more than just a rerun of a previous movement from the 1930s, the "technocrats."

As in everything, the tide comes in and the tide goes out. Night follows day and day follows night.

Their ways held sway in business for more than thirty years. But, here, as we come to the end of the first quarter of the twenty first century. Their days are now over.

The tide comes in and the tide goes out. Their day is over and new days are emerging. That is what we in our small, small way, in our small company are trying to usher in. There will be new ways of working, new ways of managing and new ways of leading.

But where to begin, especially for leadership? We can start by relying on those summed up characteristics and elements of human nature that have served humanity for thousands of years: archetypes.

First of all, what is an archetype? It is an extremely simple prototype, or example, of a personality. That could be a "goodie" or a "baddie" or a handsome prince, or a hero or a wicked stepmother or whatever. Film characters and characters in dramas and plays are made up of one or more archetypes.

For example, we love heroes, don't we? We are always in need to have someone, real or mythical to inspire us. Face it, we need people to look up to. Heroes inspire something within us to aspire to become more than just our boring, uninspiring selves and their stories help get us through the soggy, wet, dismal Wednesday in February of the soul that we all get from time to time (especially in project management, or running a company).

When I was growing up you couldn't move for tripping over heroic men and women.

They were everywhere. This country was positively dripping with them. It was a very inspiring time.

There were water, land and air speed record attempters. Spacemen, moon walkers, designers of exquisite and hideously dangerous motor cars, and aeroplanes like Concorde, the Hawker Harrier and the English Electric Lightning were flown by men who sometimes just fell out of the sky. There were also scores of psychologically damaged old men who had given their youth and their bodies as a sacrifice during the second world war - such men judged and glowered malevolently at you and were just waiting for an excuse to clip you around your ear.

Heroes? Pah. Ten a penny.

And now?…

Where have all our heroes gone? Can you see any? So who should we look up to in dark times? Political leaders? Er, no thanks, I would really rather not. (N.B. I am not being party political here. I have a special loathing for all of them, no matter what the shade).

* * *

Are there any heroes left besides the odd tech billionaire with a four storey public relations department getting them great publicity and telling us how heroic they are?

But what have archetypes got to do with us and why should it matter to us and our teams?

Well, it's a question of character, as in:

1. What sort of character and characteristics should we aspire to for ourselves as a leader?

2. What sort of character and characteristics would our team wish we had if they had a choice?

Do you think they would like us to be honorable, brave, resolute and honest? Or dishonorable, cowardly, irresolute, and dishonest?

I think we can guess, can't we?

Yet where in public and provate life do we get to see the ones we want and need? We can't.

No matter, and this is the point, we will not bother look to our current 'leaders' for guidance, luckily, we have our past and so shall be able to look to the old heroes.

The Greeks have some pretty heroic stories. Best of all, Greek heroes are all so very human, and so deeply, deeply flawed. And they nearly all failed.

But they tried.

Have a look at Odysseus, Achilles. For thinkers, try Socrates, Thrasymachus and Plato.

Let's be clear, we are never going to be as heroic as any of the above. But in a time of change where we don't see any contemporaries to inspire us, we can use their characters as inspiration, and aspire.

* * *

I think it beats looking to the behaviour of politicians. How about you?

Encouragement and Enthusiasm

Encouragement is a complex word. As I have said elsewhere, the root of the word is, "coeur," which is Norman French for heart.

Your courage comes from your heart.

Think of the middle ages English king, Richard, Coeur de Lion - Richard the lion heart.

To En-courage someone means literally, to give them heart. And the opposite is true of the word discourage, or to take away heart.

Here's an obvious question with an easy answer: do you think human beings work better when they are in an environment where they are encouraged, or when they are discouraged?

It is not a hard question, is it? The answer is obvious: people work better and more productively when they are being encouraged.

But how many bosses have you worked for who actively use discouragement as a tool of control over the people they lead and manage? It is not a management tool to increase productivity, it is simply a power play on behalf of the inadequate manager.

In the very early part of my career, I worked for lots of bosses like that. It is a little better now but there are still SO many bosses like that. Their goal is to raise their status and diminish yours.

As I have said elsewhere, a lot of our work is in setting up new teams on behalf of our clients to do projects with people who are highly talented and experienced, are from all over the world and so have rarely worked together before. One of the things we pride ourselves on is creating teams that gel together quickly, get stuff done quickly, professionally and to a really high standard. What is our secret sauce?

I give them encouragement, I inject enthusiasm every day and I foster belief in themselves. You give a group of individuals these simple things and they will soon grow into a team tht will move mountains, even if they were not what the company regards as "Stars", or "A players."

I mean, it's so basic and obvious, right? If you want to motivate a team of people, one of the best first things you can do is to encourage them individually and promote enthusiasm in the team.

It's basic common sense, isn't it?

Unfortunately, as the old cliche goes, common sense is not that common.

It is rare, as is the use of encouragement.

So please, use encouragement in your role as a leader. It is one of the most powerful tools at your disposal to promote productivity, and also make you, and the people in your team have a much , much better day.

Not only that but to bad managers who use discouragement as a tool, it is nearly always an invisible thing to them: they won't be able to see that you are using it, even when you point it out to them.

Our best waking hours are those we spend at work. We swap them for money. If those are our best hours of our day doesn't it make sense to try and make them the best they can be?

Well, the great thing about encouragement is that it has the side effect of making going to work a much better experience for everyone, including us, which has to be a good thing, right?

The Use Of Humour

I have no idea why, but many would be leaders love to think they have "a good sense of humour," and they want to share this supposed talent with the people they lead. - Unfortunately, the truth is that they invariably really, really _don't_ have a good sense of humour. Unfortunately, few people actually do, especially those who are convinced that they do.

Humour is a totally subjective thing. One person may find one comedian funny, while another may find them irritating beyond belief.

It is the same with the subject matter that they use in their material - some people find some subjects funny, while others find exactly the same subjects teeth gratingly annoying. Even professional comedians who are building a name for themselves only try to connect with half of the audience in the room. Connecting with half the room is counted on as a roaring success. If they can achieve that then they reckon they are winning.

Or to put it another way, even professional comedians know that half the audience are not going to like them. Are we professinal comedians? So what chance do we have?

Let's be real: You are in work and you are there to do a job. That job is to be slightly apart from your team. You can be friendly but you are not their fiend.

You are definitely not there to make them laugh. After all, they know that one day, you might have to get rid of them. And that will definitely not be funny.

So my advice to you is do not attempt to be funny. It is not what your team want from you. They want leadership.

They want to respect you, and there are few things more likely to lose you your respect than you attempting to be funny. Especially if you aren't.
And, never, never, ever tell blue jokes.

* * *

For a very short time, I once advised one of the most appalling leaders I have ever met. He was a CEO of a finance company that was owned by one of the major banks. He would tell desperately unfunny blue jokes at massed staff meetings and he expected the staff to laugh, which, of course, being in a power relationship - they did. But as they laughed they laughed in that special hollow way that tells you "we are only tolerating this - there will be repercussions. We don't know when, but there will be repercussions."

So he kept telling blue jokes every week. Meanwhile, the staff were building up the most seething, boiling contempt for him. I told him to stop repeatedly because it was obvious that they were losing their respect for him.

But he knew better.

Then, one day his boss came down from London and he just couldn't resist showing off to hs boss just how much a comedian he was so he told another blue joke to the staff in front of the big boss. There and then, promptly, and very publicly, he was sacked.

If you want to be a leader, be a leader. If you want to be a comedian, go and be a comedian. The two jobs do not mix.

Decades ago, I used to do stand up comedy. It was my hobby, I enjoyed writing comedy and I was pretty good at performing it. I never once "died"on stage. When I became a leader and a manager I was given some excellent advice from the CEO. He said, "ditch comedy, or ditch your career."

So I did.

I still have the career.

LEADERS AND LEADERSHIP

From Those Who Know...

Here are some fine words on leadership by Field Marshall Montgomery, 1st Viscount of Alamein.

If you have never heard of him, he was the man ultimately in charge of the **two million men** who took part in the Normandy landings during the Second World War.

Two million men. I think that qualifies him as a leader, yes?

Here he is being interviewed in the 1960s by Lord Stephen Taylor.

Lord Stephen Taylor: "Can you use the same techniques as you used in the Army in civilian life?"

Field Marshall Montgomery: "Yes. The first thing you must do is conquer yourself . If you are going to handle men, and women too (which is much more difficult). If you are to control them, you must first learn to command and control yourself. To conquer yourself. Now I was never told that. If you can't command and control yourself, you will never be able to command other people.

If you are commanding large bodies of men, or even small bodies of men, you've got to get them with you, and feel that their best interests are in your hands, that you want nothing for yourself . You are entirely out to do the best for them. If you can do that, then men, soldiers, will follow you. Of course, all soldiers will follow a successful general, - they like it".

Inspiring words, I think you'll agree, and some wonderful secrets of leadership too. These are two that appealed to me.

1.   "The first thing you must do is conquer yourself." If only half the leaders I have met took this to heart the world would be a much better place and I would not need to have written this.

"and feel that their best interests are in your hands, that you want nothing for yourself . You are entirely out to do the best for them. If you can do that, then men, soldiers, will follow you."

You know, if you took nothing more away from this book than those two comments, you'd be well on your way to becomeing a great leader.

Not a bad start.

Remember, Thou Art Mortal[9]...

There's something very weird about leadership and management which we need to keep in the back of our minds. It is called the 'power paradox.' The power paradox attracts many to leadership who, although they have the ambition, are completely and utterly unsuited[10] to it. Unfortunately, at the same time it repels those who would be really great at it. I'm guessing that part of the reason you are reading this is because you have been repelled by would-be leaders.

Sadly, their ambitions are seldom an indicator of competence. The heady whiff of status that management offers often appeals to the worst possible instincts of the worst possible candidates. In my experience as a consultant who mentors leaders, the ratio of the good to the bad is truly awful: I'm guessing that for every, one suitable leader, at least fifty are unsuitable.

Sorry to keep droning on about this but that is why _you_ _must_ volunteer for leadership. We cannot afford any more clowns.

Here is another quote to put us in the right (i.e. a humble and modest,) frame of mind:

"The most improper job of any man, even saints, (who at any rate, were at least unwilling to take it on), is bossing other men. Not one in a million is fit for it, and least of all who seek the opportunity." - J.R.R. Tolkien (author of "The Hobbit," and "Lord Of The Rings.")

---

[9] Roman generals who had won great victories were awarded a 'triumph,' which was a victory parade through the streets of Rome. As they were being praised by the citizens, they always had a slave who whispered, "Remember thou art mortal," in their ear.

[10] As one of my students once asked me on one of my courses, "Do you mean the 'fist-magnets'?" I thought that was priceless.

* * *

See what I mean? That's the power paradox. Let's see what you and I can do to reverse this.

First: What Do We Lead? What Do We Manage?

"You manage things; you lead people." - Grace Brewster Murray Hopper[11]

Great words from Grace Hopper. Most leaders are not aware of this basic, but, fundamental idea: We use management techniques to manage the things we have to manage such as keeping the lights on or shifting us form oenour stock, our processes and our accounts. Management is planning, measuring, monitoring, co-ordinating, hiring and sacking. We use leadership techniques to lead our teams. Do that right and we will be in a better place than if we don't.

But Which Comes First? Leadership or Management?

Leadership. Leadership comes first.

If you are a loner, a a "sigma male" (the same thing in my mind), a one-man band business and you need to take on an assistant, you need to be able to lead them convincingly to help you do your business before you things get more complicated and you need to manage things, such as running a warehouse, a computer system or HR's holiday booking system. Remember, you manage things, you lead people.

Leadernomics (this book) is about leadership, the sister book, "Going Agile," is about management.

What Is Your Strategy For Leadership?

You basically have two choices: you can either _impose_ your authority

---

[11] Co-inventor of the COBOL programming language and a Commodore in the US Navy - so she would know.

and push them, like a commander does, or you can _entice_ them and pull them along into accepting you and giving you the status of leader. You do this by intriguing them with your vision, your wherewithal, your knowledge and abilities. If you do this, they will choose to _invest_ you as their leader.

The first option requires some kind of threat or actual use of force, even if it is only your personality. The second requires a great deal more work on the part of the leader (especially on themselves) but the effect is much longer lasting. Another benefit is that when the time comes for the leader to finish being the leader, it normally results in a much softer landing.

Do You Want To Be A Commander or a Leader?

A commander is different to a leader. A commander belongs to a 'Command and Control' environment, such as the military, the police or the fire service. A commander commands because they have authority, and authority comes from the veiled threat of force, such as, "do this or a) I will shoot you, or b) you will lose your job." The problem with using veiled force is it generates resentment: That is where your people do the bare minimum and only acquiesce to your demands rather than fully accepting the task.

A leader **offers** themselves to the group and the group _accepts_ them. There is a kind of dialogue or process of negotiation between the leader and the group.

So, broadly, we know there are two ways to lead people:

1.   **Commanding.** We've all had this leader/manager. The "Gene Hunt[12]." They shout at and brow beat people, like the typical old

---

[12] The guv'nor in the TV series, "Life On Mars." When I started work, every manager was a complete and utter Gene Hunt.

'Theory X[13]' manager they are. The problem with behaving like that is that your people will only *acquiesce* to your demands rather than wholehearted *accepting* them. Why should you care? Well, people who acquiesce aren't as engaged and so don't give you as much effort[14] as people who accept. We will talk about low engagement later on in the book.

They comply with demands by doing the bare minimum rather than over-delivering excellence, and worst of all, being treated badly by your boss breeds resentment. As any enlightened 'Theory Y[15]' manager or leader can tell you, there are many currencies that people at work choose to get paid in. Resentment is the most expensive currency there is.

Although it is still very common, this theory X type of leadership has one fundamental drawback: it breeds resentment, and when it comes to resentment there will *always* be a reckoning, and their resentment will be paid back at a time of *their* choosing, not yours.

2. **Leadership As A Craft**: You understand that leadership is partly knowledge of set of skills, as real as the skills of a joiner or bricklayer, and acts as a bargain or agreement between you and your people. A leader says, "I want you to do this. It may be a difficult task but the rewards in increasing your skills, greater competence, job satisfaction and money will greater than the pain of doing it. Afterwards, you will be in a better place than you are now.[16]"

---

[13] From Douglas MacGregor's classic management book, "The Human Side Of Enterprise." 1960. Theory X Managers think that people are lazy and come to work for just money.

[14] Personally, I prefer 'effort' to the HR management phrase 'engagement.'

[15] Again, From Douglas MacGregor's classic management book, "The Human Side Of Enterprise." 1960. Theory Y Managers realise that people come to work for more than just money.

[16] As a shorthand, we use the phrase, "making the juice worth the squeeze." This is a phrase we use a lot, especially in the 'Thriving Index' part of the Sprint Retrospective. - It means 'does the payback justify the effort?' I have found it is the key to motivating people and knowing how they are doing. Have you ever made own orange juice? It is delicious but what an effort! it takes two bags of oranges to get a big glass and what a mess afterwards.

* * *

You offer yourself as their leader and, hopefully, after judging whether you have the right stuff, they will accept you. Why should they accept you? Because you really know that leadership is a craft, and you also know that your people will follow you if you find out what they want, and then do your best to give it to them.

But how on earth can you _know_ what your people want?

"The Enthusiastic Employee- - How Companies Profit By Giving Workers What They Want" by David Sirota and Douglas A. Klein.

This is the very best book on people management I know, and it tells you what your people really want. Even better, not many managers have ever heard of it, or read it. I urge you to read it yourself, and then keep it in your very own management library.

Mercer-Sirota, as the company who wrote the book are now called, have been doing all sorts of employee research for seriously huge, global companies like IBM and Starbucks ever since the 1970s. During their work they have learned a thing or two about what employees want, and what they want from their employers.

According to Sirota and Klein, the three factors that are most important to staff are:

1. **Equity**
   2. **Achievement**
   3. **Camaraderie**

1. Equity:

People want to be treated with a certain fairness at work. That means getting the right recognition and reward for their efforts. They already know that there are no more jobs for life, but they do want to be treated fairly while they are there. One of the little tricks for the Scrumnast manager is to make sure your people move their own work tickets. If they did the job, then let them take the credit. The first lesson for the leader.

2. *Achievement:*

People want a sense of achievement and pride from their work and also a small measure of control, too. After all, they are spending the very best hours of their day with you. There's a reason why working in monotonous jobs in factories is described as 'soul destroying.' The second lesson for the leader.

3. *Camaraderie:*

Anyone who has read Douglas MacGregor's "The Human Side Of Enterprise" knows that people don't just come to work for the money. They also come to work for all sorts of reasons, including companionship and to be social too. Work is partly how we validate ourselves. When we meet someone new, the second question we ask them is, "And what do you do?" Human beings are tribal pack animals who thrive when well socialised and do not do well at all when isolated. In fact, some of the oldest punishments we have in all our cultures are about being pushed out from the group: Excommunication, banishment, and being outlawed.

This is the third lesson for the leader to learn and is the hardest one to achieve with remote teams.

As you probably already know, we specialise in managing remote teams. I spend as much time trying to do something to overcome the people in my remote team's sense of isolation as I do on *anything* else. If you are running a remote team do not underestimate just how big a job this is and how much responsibility rests with you as leader to get it right.

An Easy Tip: One of the most successful things I have found is to open *all* the video meetings five minutes early, so that my teams have a space where they can catch up with each other informally before the work starts. This is a simple trick I learned from working with older salesmen in my youth, who spent a great deal of time talking with potential clients about how their families were getting along before doing any hard-nosed commercial negotiations. I also encourage team members to video call each other frequently during the working day if they are working together on a task to minimise this sense of isolation.

Okay, So Now We Know What They Want At Work, But What Do They Want From Us As Leaders?

First of all, most people actually want to be led. Why? Partly because they don't want to lead because their experience tells them the eventual outcome for most leaders is not that great. When leaders get the bum's rush it is not often an elegant end.

Although they often have the ability to do so, not everyone wants to be a leader at work, and there are as many reasons why that is, as there are people. One of them being that most people want to be liked at work.

Second of all, they may want to be led, but they certainly do not want to be led by anyone who is weak, or incompetent, or without integrity, or directionless, or lacking in vision, or worst of all, uses their status to attempt to sleep with their staff.

Amongst other things, they want their leaders to be strong, ethical, to behave honourably, be of good character, have a convincing vision for the future and have confidence in their competence and their abilities to lead them there. After all, wouldn't you want that?

You may be thinking "Surely he's talking about one of those alpha type personalities, but I that is not me."

Yes, You Are. In Fact, We All Are.

This needs to be said again. All those alpha, beta, delta gamma, sigma and omega 'personality types' are not really personality types at all.

They are simply examples of different behaviours that we all exhibit in different social settings at different times.

Which one you are in any particular situation just depends on the situation. We change how we behave in different social situations.

For example, when I am leading a team or coaching a group online in leadership and management then, in that situation, I will be the alpha because I know more and am more experienced than anyone else, and I am there to mentor and generally be in charge - it's what I'm paid for and it's what people expect me to do. However, in a different social situation I won't be the one who knows more than anyone else. Then it will be extremely unlikely that I will behave as an alpha.

For example, I love to go sailing on yachts and have done for years.

However, when I was doing my RYA Day Skipper exam, I was an unqualified skipper, and I was being examined by a qualified skipper. The real skipper was ultimately in charge of the yacht and that made them the alpha.

There is no 'faking it until you make it,' self-help nonsense when at sea - get it wrong and people can die. Even when I was temporarily 'in charge' while being examined - issuing orders to the crew and had the helm, if I had messed up at any time then he would have taken charge and taken over. That made the skipper the alpha. It is the same for all of us: in certain situations, we are the alpha, in others we are not.

The Essence of Leadership

"Whether you think you can, or whether you think you can't, you're probably right." Henry Ford (allegedly)

This bit is for the skim readers among us, just in case you skipped the early bits, here's a summary: Leadership is a practical craft, not a "gift" and it isn't magical. You don't get to be a leader by doing an M.B.A. You get to be a leader by being a leader and you get better at it just by doing it.

Despite what business journalists may tell you, it is not that rare a skill.

The number of people who can lead a group of people is a *lot* bigger than you would imagine. Outside of work, people are already involved in leadership and management. They are leading clubs and making life changing decisions about themselves and their families every single day without any permission from your H.R. department.

We have all worked for someone who is an awful leader. First of all, we need to make a distinction between a leader and someone in authority. People in authority may not be good leaders.

Second, we need to distinguish between leadership and ownership. Just because the third-generation idiot son of the founder is your boss, it really does not follow they will be a good leader.

The real leaders in any group are the individuals that everyone turns to when it all goes wrong. Often, just after the people who should be in charge have been found to be lacklustre. Again.

True leaders have natural authority and trust in a group, even if they don't appear on the organisation chart. After all, Winston Churchill was Winston Churchill <u>before</u> he became Prime Minister of wartime Britain.

* * *

Those ambitious, thrusting types sharp elbowing their way to the front all by themselves? They may be the very people that we in the organisation have to watch out for most.

The Reluctant Leader? Who Are They?

We will talk more about reluctant leaders later, but for now, let's introduce oursleves to them.

They are all around us yet are often overlooked. Why can they make good leaders?

1. Because they often see their role of leadership as being part of something bigger than just being about them, which is great for those they lead.

2. They often know themselves quite well: both the good and the bad parts. That allows them to be honest about their weaknesses and so want to continue to develop.

3. Knowing that they are themselves lacking in strengths, often means they are happy to invest in other people's training and development.

4. They don't tend to be pompous and entitled (which is both a really, really good thing and makes a rather wonderful change).

5. They tend to lead with quiet authority, rather than leading by having tantrums and 'terrible twos.'

6. They also tend to be genuine people of substance, rather than people of style and flim-flam.

7. They tend to lack big egos, and so tend to put more trust in evidence than trust their own, or others, eminence or expertise.

8. Above all, because of their experiences of being led badly themselves, what makes them hesitant about putting themselves forward is that they REALLY don't want to be a BAD leader.

* * *

There's a long tradition for the reluctant leader. How about George Washington, Moses, Mahatma Gandhi, and Pope Francis? When newly elected, the new Speaker of the House of Commons is dragged reluctantly to the Speaker's chair.

The Intriguing Leader

Here's a secret that reluctant leaders know in their bones: the secret of leading is not about foisting yourself on them, it is about learning how to get your people to *follow* you.

That requires that you have it within you for people to turn to you with confidence, consider thoughtfully what you are saying and doing, and then commit to invest their time, effort and skills in their putting their future with you.

How do you do that? Partly by intriguing them. You supply your group with a vision of the future that is both evocative for them and worthwhile to *them*. How? By leaving space. The vision must allow them to fill in some of the blanks for themselves. When your people fill in the blanks for themselves, they take your vision, and make it their own by putting their own interpretation onto it. They begin to own it for themselves.

But a vision is not enough. You must inspire them with confidence that you have the wherewithal and heft to defend them from both above, and from the sides. They want and need a champion, not a friend.

Fear, Dread, and Doubt, And The True Leader

If the thought of leading a group of people fills you with dread, then good - You are just the sort of person your people need.

Those nerves in your stomach mean you already have one of the best pre-qualifications there is to become an excellent leader. Those nerves will help to raise your game and your judgement for your people. Good judgement is essential for a great leader.

You may not think so, but ask any actor, comedian or musician: when you need to perform, your nerves make you do your job better. You just need to accept them.

Not a single first day of a project has ever gone by when I have had to begin to lead a new team full of hope and promise, or turn around a gang of disgruntled, dysfunctional, low performers into a group of up-and-at-em high achievers, that I haven't felt 'that feeling' in the pit of my stomach. And just about everyone is the same. So, if you're nervous at the prospect of leadership, don't worry. That's actually a *really* good sign.

Here's another thing you should ask of an actor, comedian or musician. Ask them, which is harder to play to, a small audience or a huge audience? Easy answer, right? The big crowd must the harder gig. Wrong, it's actually the small audience.

Big audiences give bigger applause and bigger laughs because of something called social proof.[17] Social proof is when a lot of people look around them at the lots of other people around them and say to themselves "well, they must be good: look at all the other people here. They can't be wrong." The hardest audience to play to is the small audience. It is the same with leading. The hardest group to lead is actually a small group. If you can lead a small group, you can lead a big group.

With the right attitude, knowledge and training, almost everyone [18] can lead.

And there are a lot more leaders in the world than you would think. They are all around us. Just because they aren't leading right now in

---

[17] This is the original meaning of social proof, not the thing that internet marketers talk about these days.

[18] But not everyone. Especially not those rather 'odd' people in your workplace who think that doing things with spreadsheets and slide software is real work or like real life. i think that'a why they are called technocrats…

the thing you are all involved in, doesn't mean they are not a leader. They may be already leading in all sorts of ways outside of work.

More than that, I have taught many people leadership who are not leading in work, and have not put themselves forward for leadership *precisely* because they are leading very worthwhile projects *outside* of work. They lead elsewhere.

Only the unwise would ignore that potential for leadership - so, as part of your leadership, you really have to find out what your people are doing outside work. I have often been amazed at the leadership talent (and modesty) displayed by sometimes very humble team members.

As I have always told my Leadernomics students

- You <u>Know</u> When You Can Lead - It's In Your Bones

And you know, don't you?

Offering Them Some<u>one</u> Worth Following

True Leaders Have a Vision:

A vision is a 'reason why,' (or as Nietzsche would have said, a 'strong why,') your people should follow you and your ideas.

A vision is just a plan with a purpose. The successful leader always has a vision of the future that is better and looks further forward than the vision (or lack of vision) that everyone else can see. After all, why should anyone follow you if the future you are offering them is worse than the future they think they could achieve without you? They won't.

Try this vision for size…

Why is Martin Luther King's "I have a dream," speech still so inspiring today, sixty-odd years after he made it? Because he dreamed of a so much better future for his followers than they could see themselves.

Even though knew he would not see it himself, when Doctor King said, "I may not get there with you," he was telling them this future was about *them*, not *him*.

Leaders know where they are going. It may be a little blurry at the edges but they are very confident that it will be a better place than where they are now, or where they have come from. They can inspire others that it will be worth the sacrifices that were made so they get there.

Their vision is clear, they have thought it through and turned it into words that when spoken, it inspires others. It makes enough sense to those that hear it that they become convinced that it is a rational choice to bet on this better future.

The key to a Vision Statement:

Above all, the vision must be a short and snappy thing, saying it all in the fewest words possible.

(That's why an expensive, four-page "Mission Statement" produced by an expensive consultancy company just doesn't cut the mustard).

Some Examples (feel free to steal)

The Positive Approach:

"To Build The Best (product/service) in the top end of the GB market so that our customers constantly sing our praises which helps sell to our future customers."

The Negative Approach:

"To subvert the existing…"

Here's one my team came up with during a lockdown project in the UK. We had six months to procure and deliver 500,000 laptops, tablets and internet connectivity to the poorest schoolchilden in England. It was made up of a consortium of Global 500 companies, government, schools and my team of Ruby programmers. Lots of pressure and lots of egos. This is what we came up with:

"To subvert the effects of Covid on the most vulnerable children in England by giving them the best tools for their schooling, knowing that, among them, there just may be… another young Einstein."

Did it work? Well, we delivered 550,000 machines in four months. You tell me whether you think it had an effect or not. I think it did.

* * *

True Leaders Can Prioritise

Good leaders can do this, and bad leaders can't. But it is a vital ability for any leader. Why? For three reasons:

1.   It makes decision making MUCH easier. You have a list. You organise it, top to bottom, in order of importance. Which item will you do first? You do the one at the top of the list. Which one will you do second? The second one. If you run out of money, you will have done the most important things. The end.

2.   The people you are leading need direction. They need to know which thing to do first, what to do second, and so on. It is unfair to ask them to make the decision when it is your decision to make.

3. As a leader you will always have limited resources, and there will always be unlimited demands placed upon them. You may be asked to do everything and more - but you can't. The most vital things is to achieve are the most important things, otherwise you may put your team in danger of achieving nothing. What we are trying to avoid here is doing 'busy work:' that is, activity for the sake of activity. Busy work is the stuff that looks like productive work but isn't. Look around you at your clients and competitors, there are lots of jobs that are wholly consumed with doing busy work. There are very few things as expensive as busy work. But that's okay, because while _they_ are burning resources, _you_ will not be.

Prioritisation is a difficult skill to learn for the new leader or manager.

After all, up until becoming a leader or manager, your whole job has been about completing _all_ the tasks you have been given by your bosses.

If you complete them all you get praised - if you don't complete them then you get asked an uncomfortable, "why not?" Suddenly, everything has changed - you have to pick and choose what you are going to do instead of doing everything, and that change in mentality is difficult to square with the history of your entire work life up to now.

Not everyone makes that transition. You can tell those who have not made the change by their anguished howls of, "but it's _all_ important!"

Unfortunately, it just isn't. And unfortunately, they are condemned to a career in middle management until they do. But not you, Scrumnast. Not you.

Some Prioritisation Techniques[19]:

Prioritising by Value.[20] To do this properly, the first thing you need is a real idea of the proposed value and cost of each of the items that you intend to make (regardless of whether you are building products or services, having sight of budgets makes _everything_ easier to manage and control).

Secondly, take the list and rank it in order of value.

Thirdly, you need to know how much your team costs to run in total (the 'run rate'), per week or per month.

The run rate for the team, together with the estimated value of the next additional thing, give you a 'decision gate.' What that means is, if the value of the next thing on the list is greater than the team's run rate, then you can go ahead and do it. If the value is lower than the run rate of the team then you don't.

There will come a time when you have completed all the most valuable items, and you have arrived at a 'Minimum Viable Product[21].'

---

[19] There are, of course MANY others. These are the ones I tend to use more than any other.

[20] My personal favourite. It seems to put everyone at their ease more than any other technique because it just makes sense to normal people to do the most valuable things first.

[21] Imagine you are making ice cream. The Minimum Viable Product (MVP) is a plain vanilla ice cream. No raspberry sauce, no chopped nuts, no sprinkles and no flake. It is some complete stand-alone product that your clients can buy but has no bells or whistles, or any go-faster stripes.'

But you may still have some budget left. What to do? Should you continue adding bells and whistles, or do you make a value judgement and say, "we're done"? I work with a lot of marketing companies, so their preference is to stop and see if the basic product sells as it is. If it does then carry on. If it doesn't then you give the money back from the budget.

Top Three - What Do You Have To Achieve Today?

This is a good method when you are not in a position to know the budget numbers, or when you are in a steady state of work where little is changing.

I once spent three months mentoring a potentially excellent new leader who had been promoted on a "let's see if they sink or swim," basis. He had all the attributes you need to become an excellent leader, apart from his lack of ability to prioritise. This was threatening his ability to swim, and his career.

I had him draw up a to do list with three things for the day that he actually _had_ to achieve. Once he had achieved all three of them, he could draw up another three things but not before. It took a little time for him to get used to it, but once the behaviour became ingrained, he became an excellent, and very rounded leader.

MoSCoW prioritisation:

The "**MoSCoW**" acronym stands for "**M**ust have, **S**hould have, **C**ould have, **W**on't have." It is an old-school PRINCE2 project manager's technique for prioritising what you are planning to do and what you won't be doing. You take all the attributes that your product could have, and you decide which bucket they will go in. Every product must have certain things, there will be some that it should have, some that it could have and some that it definitely won't have. This technique is still widely used to decide what will be in scope for the development of project, and what will be out of scope.

* * *

True Leaders Can Organise

You won't last long as a leader if you rely on your charisma at the expense of your organisation skills. Chaotic leaders do not last long, no matter how charismatic they may be.

True Leaders Set The Tone

Emotional tone is important. Your positive, confident manner, how you carry yourself and your energy are infectious.

Your team will always take their mood from you. They look to you for all sorts of visual cues and clues to how things are going, especially how they are going outside the team. If you are being positive, then they will be positive.

But if you are nervous, they will be nervous. And nothing slows down the productivity of a team more than unsettling nervous agitation, especially if they don't know why you are nervous. Remember, as a leader, you are permanently on display. You must be mindful of your demeanour at all times, but especially when things are not going well. A bad atmosphere is contagious and can run through the team and affect everyone in it in no time at all.

True Leaders Have What the Team Judge To Be Good Character - Personal Qualities Of The True Leader:

It helps if the True Leader has, on average, more of the characteristics and attributes that the tribe or group value than the individuals in the tribe or group have at the moment.

You definitely need to be strong, but you don't need to be the strongest in the tribe. After all, you need to let others have some space to excel themselves.

* * *

You need energy, but you don't need to be the most energetic.

You need to be smart, but you don't need to be the smartest in the tribe.

You need good judgement, but you don't need to be a judge.

It's who you are in the round that counts most of all.

Above all, you need courage, and you need to tell the truth.

Leaders are decisive. They don't dither or faff about.

Leaders make things right when they have gone wrong. They have the strength to apologise when they realise they have done wrong.

Most of these positive qualities are needed, but all are needed in moderation, especially if they begin to harm the other traits that are more highly prized. For example, you must definitely be enthusiastic and energetic, but if you let your enthusiasms affect your judgement, they will drop you like a stone.

Offering Them Something Worth Following

Offer them a reason why, something worthwhile to invest their time in and follow and something that lends the work a purpose.

Adults need a good reason why to do anything well. A good reason why gives _purpose_, and that is crucial if you want great quality work, done on time and done within budget.

Everyone wants a better future for themselves and their loved ones. It is a simple reason they want to be in a better position than they are at the moment. You need to give them a credible reason why they should believe that following you will make that happen.

* * *

You need to give them reasons why they should follow you. You need to have a combination of methods, plans, and confidence that is better than the plan they have in their head. Give them a great way of working. Luckily, you will learn that in the Scrum section of the book.

Integrity: Competency, Character and Commitment

Competency is knowing and showing that you can organise people and things well. This mean that they can be confident that if they work with you, they can achieve a better life than they are enjoying now.

Character: your character is judged by your actions: what you say and what you do. The people that you want to follow you want you to have at least as much integrity as they do. More is better. in the way they go about life. And they have every right to expect that from you. After all, they are investing their future livelihoods with you.

Commitment: Are you a sort of person who will stand steadfast and strong when things go awry? Or are you a fly-by-night character who will disappear at the first obstacle? Will you bind to your people and are you truly committed to the future vision you're offering? Will you balance that with being open to change when the evidence shows you need to change course?

And you need to show that you can do all these things because there are so many bad leaders and managers in the world.

Even when it is done well, leadership and management is the least efficient activity in your organisation, and that little nugget comes from the Harvard Business Review.

What's worse, they also say, "65% of managers add zero or negative net value to the company."

We had better make sure we know how to do it properly, because our teams already know all there is to know about bad leaders.

Toyota and True Leadership

I'm a huge admirer of Toyota and their leadership and management philosophies. These are all bound up in the "Toyota Way," and the "Toyota Production System." Everything you will read in every book on them tells you they are the ultimate in producing practical, pragmatic, productive people.

One of the many interesting features of Toyota, (and many Japanese companies) is that, unlike companies in the west, they grow their leaders from their own staff rather than buying them in.

Toyota have fourteen management principles. The ninth principle says, *"Grow Leaders Who Thoroughly Understand the Work, Live the Philosophy, And Teach It To Others."*

There you go. Common sense really. Pick someone you have known all their professional working lives or pay a head-hunter a bucket of money to go and find you someone who may, or may not, change your company for the better. I know which option I would rather pick if I could.

But leadership in Toyota is very different to how we might think of leadership in the west. Here's a quote from Alex Warren, who is a former Senior Vice President of Toyota Motor Manufacturing, at their Kentucky plant:

"Until management gets their egos out of the way and goes to the whole team and leads them all together … senior management will continue to miss out on the brain power and extraordinary capabilities of all their employees. At Toyota, we simply place the highest value on our team members and do the best we can to listen to them and incorporate their ideas into our planning process."

Remember that quotation that I saw on the wall of Panasonic Europe from Konosuke Matsushita? Strikingly similar, aren't they?

* * *

What are some of the characteristics of Toyota's management (and other Japanese companies) that we have seen and what makes them so powerful?

They grow their leaders from within, what are the benefits of that?

They don't pay fortunes to head hunters to find them management 'rock stars' who may have a completely different ethos to the company.

That means there is more consistency in sticking with the long-standing company philosophy and they avoid the 'whip sawing' effect of changing focus and direction every few years. Their people know where they are.

Here's an example:

I got into Lean management whilst working at Panasonic Europe in 1995. On about the third week of my work with there, Ikuo, the Japanese manager and I were talking during a work break. I asked him if Japanese managers ever moved between Japanese companies. He simply said, "no."

When I asked him why that was, he said, "My grandfather operated machinery in the Matsushita (Panasonic) factory, my father was an engineer in the Matsushita factory, and I am a manager at Matsushita. My grandson will be a vice president."

Well, if you are working at "Take The Money and Run UK (2015) Ltd," how does that sound? Naive? Well, hardly. Matsushita has a 250-year business plan and *everyone* who worked for them knew about it. If you have a business plan that stretches for 250 years, then that gives a worker a certain faith and confidence that they are part of something larger and worthwhile.

Compare that with the life expectancy of a British limited company. Of every company that starts out this year, 80% will be out of business within five years. And that was before the pandemic.

* * *

But why can't we have 250-year business plans in Britain? It obviously makes a statement that all your people can commit to. It also leaves the leaders with the idea that they are custodians, not masters of the universe, and that a good part of their duty is to deliver their company to those yet to come in a robust and stable condition.

What's the point of telling you this? Well, leadership is definitely not the same thing everywhere you look, different forms of leadership can bring about very different outcomes and we can learn a lot from them.

Oh, and just in case you're thinking that these are Japanese companies with a long histories of Samurai traditions, and being British, we can't do that kind of thing here, most Japanese management thinking actually emerged from the work of an American called William Edwards Deming, who worked in Japan in the 1950s.

Reluctant Leaders: The Last Overlooked Resource in Organisations.

We are going to look at this form the point of view of something called succession planning. Every successful leader as their organisation grows needs to think about it.

In essence, it means: where are tomorrow's leaders coming from?

It is a big question for the successful leader because if their organisation grows quickly, they have to go up the ladder too. Otherwise it will not be long before you will become extended beyond what you can cope with - and that happens a lot.

As you go up the ladder you will need to backfill your old job with one or more replacements. What we as Scrumnasts are looking for, is a source that others may not be used to using.

Human Resources departments have no problem whatsoever identifying the standard 'brand X^{22},' ambitious, sharp-elbowed, traditional manager. After all, these charmers tend to self-identify themselves through their ambition, drive and general 'Draco Malfoy[23]'-ism.

But what you may not have heard is that there is a *terrible* attrition rate amongst managers and leaders. Most of them don't last very long at all. Why? Well, and I know I have said this elsewhere, but it is **<u>important.</u>** According to the Harvard Business Review, more than 65% of managers make 'zero or negative contribution' to their organisations. Worse than that, 65% of managers last less than six months before they are 'let go.'

* * *

---

[22] Not quite theory X, but close…
[23] Oh come on, you've read Harry Potter…

And 'let-go' they are. I have seen it a lot, and it is never a happy day.

Worse, often, it's not only them that gets fired when they get the push. It's normally complete carnage throughout their department too.

It doesn't end there, either. Don't forget that those managers who got fired have no other choice but to go and get a management job somewhere else. *Some* will have used the experience and learned to manage well, but most won't. There's a good living to be had for employment agencies who place bad managers in companies. A sobering thought.

As one of my students told me recently on one of our online management courses, "First, they only promote you onto the management ladder because you are the best in the department at your job. But then, they leave you on your own to work everything out for yourself. If you don't, they just get the next person in line."

Which means that there is a never-ending need for **_GOOD_** leadership and management.

Where is it to come from? And where are HR departments looking for it? Not externally. Not any longer. It is not only expensive to search of outside 'talent,' it is a very risky business. Instead, they have begun to look for them internally, inside the organisation. Why? It is cheaper and less risky because they are dealing with known quantities. They even have a name for them now, they call them the 'low-flyers.'

These are the people who have more than just the talent and the ability, but who take the responsibility of leading and managing so seriously that they would rather not do it than be bad at it. It daunts them. Good. The prospect of leading a team is supposed to be daunting. It's the ones who are not daunted by it you should beware of

The daunted? These are the reluctant types.

Ambitious types? Better take note that the good ones are coming to replace you. Reluctantly, but they are coming.

* * *

Why Is A Reluctant Leader So Appealing?

Because they often see their role of leadership as being part of something bigger than just being about them, which is both great for those they lead and for the organisation. It's a good bet you haven't bought a psychopath.

They have a certain maturity and often know themselves quite well: both the good and the bad parts.

That allows them to be honest about their weaknesses and so want to continue to develop.

Knowing that they are themselves lacking in strengths, often means they are happy to invest in other people's training and development.

They don't tend to be stereotypically pompous and entitled (which is a really, really good thing and makes a rather refreshing and wonderful change).

They tend to lead with quiet authority, rather than leading by shouting, screaming, having tantrums and showing they never progressed beyond the "terrible twos."

They also tend to be people of substance, rather than people of style and flim-flam.

They tend to lack big egos, and so tend to put more trust in the evidence before their eyes than trusting their own, or others, expertise and eminence.

Above all, because of their experiences, what makes them hesitant about putting themselves forward is that they REALLY don't want to be is a BAD leader.

There's quite a tradition of the reluctant leader in the wider world: How about George Washington, Moses, Mahatma Gandhi, and Pope Francis? When newly elected, the new Speaker of the House of

Commons makes a great show[24] of being dragged reluctantly to the Speaker's chair. If you are reluctant, you're in some great company and there's a good history behind you

---

[24] Okay, I know I am over-egging this, they are never _that_ reluctant…

Leadership Sometimes Depends Upon Looking Through The Right End Of The Telescope

Figure 2 When You Have To Lead A Group Of People, It Is A Lot Easier If You Make Sure You Are Looking Through The Right End Of The Telescope...

Look through the wrong end of a telescope and an astonishingly useful tool becomes perfectly useless. It doesn't do its job.

Which just goes to show that having a tool is not enough - you have to learn to use the tool properly for it to be useful.

It is not that the telescope is broken, it is still working perfectly. It is simply that the user does not know how to use it and anyone who knows about telescopes and sees you looking through the wrong end, will know you are an idiot.

* * *

Leadership is very similar: for it to work properly you have to know how to use the right tools in the right way. That means be familiar with the tool and look throught it from the right way round.

True leaders know look through the right end of the telescope. They know that the trick is not so much to try to lead people, it is to do the right things in the right order so that people want to *follow them.*

The second trick is that true leaders know that most people want, and in fact *need,* to have someone to follow.

Being a leader is hard. Having everyone look to you when things go wrong and you needing to come up with the right answer and be quick about is not easy. It does not appeal to everyone. But then, few people are actually asked to be leaders, most need to volunteer.

To be sure there are rules that people apply to their leaders, but they are not that hard to live up to.

The Ambitious Leader Versus The Reluctant Leader:

Most ambitious leaders lead from the point of view that, if they charge off into the future, people will follow them because they are convinced their mixture of personal charisma, animal magnetism and dynamism are irresistible. If only.

Of course, this actually works for those rare individuals who *genuinely* possess such talents. Unfortunately, for every single person who truly was born to be a natural leader, there seem to be about twenty or thirty who are just truly convinced they were. The problem is not the true leader, - they will always emerge - it is the thirty deluded ones who think they are true leaders that we have to clear up after.

In comparison, reluctant leaders know a little secret: **people will always want the best future they can get**. Why would they want anything else? If a leader can conjure up a vision of a better and more appealing future for their people than they already have, then people will naturally follow them (as long as they are convinced that that person they are about to follow also has the wherewithal to deliver it).

In other words, they look at leadership through the *right* end of the telescope.

Your People Want A Good Now, - But They Want A Better Future More

Why is it that people commit completely to certain leaders and are left cold by others?

Why would they leave an almost certain future where they are, and change jobs for an unknown environment?

Why change from what you know to embark on a risky future?

The answer? Self-interest: People want a better future for themselves and their loved ones. Although they like a good 'now,' they are willing to trade a sure not very good now for the promise of a better future.

The same thing goes for voting for governments, life partners, cars and career changes.

So, if we give them a pretty okay now and give them confidence that their future will be even better than that if they stick with you, we can be confident that they will follow us.

It is always worth remembering this every time just before you open your mouth as a manager or leader. They are not following you because of your magnetic personality; they are following you because you are the best game in town.

Which means that you had better be on top of your game, because other games may be available.

Giving Your People A *Now* Worth Following

How can you *know* what your people want so that you can give it to them?

You could either ask them directly, or you could read the results of the work of some very clever people whose only job is to ask employees what they really want from their work, who then give the anonymised results back to the client.

That's what I did.

Who would I ask? *The Sirota Institute.* And I have. Why? Because I think they are the best at that sort of thing.

The Sirota Institute have been doing employee research for seriously huge global companies such as IBM and Starbucks since the 1970s and they wrote a book.

The book is called *"The Enthusiastic Employee, How Companies Profit By Giving Their Employees What They Want,"* and it is by David Sirota, Louis A. Mishkind, and Michael Irwin Meltzer.

Buy it. Read it. It will make you a better leader.

So, What Do Your People Want? - Equity, Achievement, and Camaraderie

We have already spoken about Sirota book's recommendations for treating your staff with Equity, Achievement, and Camaraderie. But the issue is *so* important, and so often overlooked, I think it needs hammering home again and again. So, once again:

1.   Equity:

It turns out people want to be treated with a certain fairness at work.

Who would have thought? Equity to them means getting the right recognition and reward for their efforts. They already know that there are no more jobs for life but they do want to be treated fairly while they are there and working for you. This is the first lesson for the reluctant leader.

2.   Achievement:

Apparently, people want a sense of achievement and pride from their work and also a small measure of control, too. Why not, after all, they are spending the very best hours of their day with you. There's a reason why working in monotonous jobs in factories is described as 'soul destroying.' It often has no purpose for the people doing it, and we all need purpose. This is the second lesson for the reluctant leader.

3.   Camaraderie:

People don't just come to work for the money. They also come to work for the company and to be social. Human beings are tribal pack animals who thrive when well socialised and do not do well when isolated. In fact, some of the oldest punishments are about being pushed out from the group:

Ex-communication, banishment, and being outlawed. This is the third lesson for the reluctant leader and the hardest one to achieve with remote teams. How to instil that feeling that it is great to be in this group?

One of the biggest problems with working with remote teams is fostering that sense of _belonging_. I spend a great deal of my time on getting this this right with my own teams and it pays dividends. In the absence of anyone else to do it, that is our responsibility.

Of course, a lot of this is forgotten knowledge. Actually, we have known much of this ever since Douglas Murray McGregor wrote his classic, and excellent management book "The Human Side Of

Enterprise[25]," which he wrote in 1960.

Sometimes, the secrets of the world are hidden in plain sight.

One of the biggest issues to address in working with remote teams is fostering that sense of belonging to a group. In the absence of anyone else to do it, we have to make it our responsibility. We need to pay special attention[26] to this when we work remotely.

At Scrumnastics, we have added these three ethics to the five Scrum ethics that we use and, to be honest, we have put them _above_ the standard Scrum ethics because our teams prefer them.

Giving Your People a _Future_ worth Following

How do you give your people a better bet on the future?

You give them a 'postcard of the destination,' - a vision of a better future: a great reason "_why_?"

Why? Because a great 'reason why,' or a 'strong why[27],' lends your quest a _purpose_, and people crave a purpose.

A great, well thought out, reasoned "why we are doing this?" is crucial because, in an often seemingly random world, a sense of purpose gives your people a reason to commit to, and share in, your dream.

Here's the best 'reason why,' I have ever seen:

____

[25] "The Human Side Of Enterprise," is another book I urge you to buy and read. It will not only teach you about "Theory X," and "Theory Y" managers, but it will make you a better manager of people.
[26] For that I use the Daily Scrum, to start off the day together, the "Sharpening the Tools," to close the working day together and the Sprint Retrospective, the Sprint debriefing session. Some Scrum Masters think that doing games helps, I do not.
[27] "He who has a why can endure any how." – Frederick Nietzsche

* * *

"This country should commit itself to achieving the goal, before this decade is out, of landing a man on the moon and returning him safely to earth." John F. Kennedy 1961.

Now that is a cracking reason why, isn't it? I especially like the "and returning him safely to earth" bit. That's what I call really classy.

The most persuasive purposes have the following characteristics of being specific, measurable, assignable (or actionable), realistic and timely. You may know this as the "SMART" acronym.

The fact that President Kennedy's beautiful words also conformed beautifully to the traditional S.M.A.R.T. Management acronym for a goal is probably not a co-incidence.

As you probably already know, S.M.A.R.T. stands for **Specific, Measurable, Assignable, Realistic and Timely.**

1. Specific: " the goal,… of landing a man on the moon and returning him safely to earth."

2. Measurable: Before: We have never been to the moon. After: Oh yes we have. And we can go again.

3. Assignable: Who? "**This nation** should commit itself to …"

4. Realistic: Was it realistic? Well, they achieved it, and they achieved it within a decade. Sometimes, even the most breathtakingly audacious goals can be achieved.

5. Timely: "before this decade is out."

In fact, they did better than that. NASA took three men to the moon and put two men on the moon, and brought all three of them safely back, in July 1969. Heroic.

The vision of the future is the reason why, Nietzsche's 'strong why,' from all the possible things that the members of your team could possibly do with their time, they should care enough to go with you from where they are now to where you imagine they could be. A shared vision is a transformative thing.

The reason I mention SMART acronym is that when you are stuck for a purpose, SMART gives you a great test for any ideas you may have. If it passes the SMART test, it is very likely that your idea of a purpose will be a winner with your people.

That's the strong why, the reason why.

Recap: Giving Your People Some*one* Worth Following

Remember that as a leader, you are not their friend, you are their champion.

You are not there to be David Brent from "The Office." They know that you pretending to be their best mate is simply a manipulative lie, and they will despise you for it. Although they will not show it, they will seethe inside. There will be a reckoning.

The key to being a champion is to have, on average, more of the good personality characteristics that your people admire than they do. They want you to be the person they wish they could be.

It's who you are in the round that counts most of all, but you had better know that you have:

Wherewithal:

No-one wants to follow someone who is floppy and the flaccid for very long. Why would they? Would you?

Instead, you need to show you have that certain 'wherewithal.' That combination of drive, confidence, grit, vision and "Oomph," that they don't, or more likely, can't, show in work. You demonstrating these qualities is what gives them the courage to have faith in you that you will deliver the vision you gave them. This is part of you being their champion.

* * *

You also need to realise and be aware just how hard it is to be a subordinate, and, just how hard it is for perfectly capable, mature people to *be* subordinate in work. Outside of work they may lead families, voluntary groups or lead and manage all manner of wonderful things, but in work they have to kowtow to people who they may well have no respect for as people. Be someone they can respect. It will make a difference.

The Ability To Speak Truth To Power:

You do need to be able to serve them as a shield against those from above them. Again, this is part of being their champion.

They need to know that you will be batting for them as individuals and battling for them as a team. I have led many teams composed of the most red-blooded, hairy-chested individuals who make you think "wow, I bet he's afraid of nobody!" Yet, when it comes to talking with a bunch of weedy guys with better suits and higher status, they simply wither when confronted by them.

It's not even limited to physicality. I have led a team of PhD maths wizards who were brighter than the sun, yet they shrivelled in front of a bunch of sharp, shrewd, but ultimately much thicker blokes who had (fake) posh accents.

You need to be smart, but you don't need to be the smartest in the group.

You definitely need to be strong, but you don't need to be the strongest.

But you do need to be strong enough. And have the courage to tell the truth to power. There are too many lily-livered liars masquerading as leaders living among us. Our teams expect better than that and they deserve better from their leaders.

Great leaders are decisive. They may take time to take counsel from their people but when they have come to a decision they implement swiftly. They don't dither or faff about once a decision has to be made.

Great leaders also make things right when they have gone wrong. They also have the strength to apologise when they realise they have done wrong.

But that's fine, to err is human.

Now, Scrumnast, go and be a _great_ leader.

The Servant Leader

At Scrumnastics, we use a method of project managing based on something called Scrum. We actually add quite a few extra things as well but the core is definitely Scrum. In Scrum, they split management and leadership into two distinct 'roles.' The leadership role, or in Scrum's words, the 'accountability,' is called the Scrum Master.

Traditionally, the Scrum Master was always described as a 'servant leader.' (Although they have extended the role to being a 'true leader,' the foundation is still that of a servant leader).

That meant that they do everything from keeping the team and the work running, using the best Scrum traditions, acting as an ambassador for Scrum throughout the organisation, being a 'fixer,' and being an all-round good egg.

They serve the team by using their valuable skills in order to lead their teams. Of course, this description of what needs to happen in the role is not new. In your grandparents' time, whoever had this role would have been called the foreman.

Actually, the idea of a servant leader exists outside of Scrum. Captains of sport teams lead by serving as well as shouting, and anyone who has a background in going to church will be very familiar with the idea. Pastors, vicars and priests all act as servant leaders, and it's the same with all sorts of community groups.

There is also a huge body of work in formal management study about what a servant leader does and how every company needs them. Unfortunately, when people hear the term, they tend to just hear the word servant and not leader.

But actually, and occasionally, every leader needs to be a servant leader. It goes with the job.

What Does It Mean To Be A "Servant Leader?"

* * *

Here's a practical example of what a Servant Leader does and is. We will use a traditional work team of house builders and their foreman.

Foreman is a very old term for a leader of a team of people with various different skills, such as you would see on a building site. 'Foreman' is short for the foremost man in the group.

You Don't Need To Do "Scrum" To Be A Servant Leader: Bryn's Builders:

The term servant leader is not exclusively part of Scrum. It stands alone and is used in many different management frameworks.

Here's an example where some burly chested builders might use it.

Imagine, it's halfway through the working day on a building site when the joiner tells the foreman that he is about to run out of screws, and he wants to go and get some more from the building supplies merchant.

The wily foreman knows that if the carpenter goes off site, he is likely to get sidetracked for the rest of the day and it will be unlikely that he will be back on the building site today. This means the team's progress on the house building (that the foreman is ultimately responsible for,) will slow down or even stop:

That's not a great option.

Instead, the foreman offers to go and get some from the suppliers, knowing that the carpenter has just enough screws for a few more hours work, which will be enough to keep him going until he returns.

This means that the carpenter is able to carry on working in the meantime and the team won't fall behind because of any work that they are relying on from the carpenter not getting finished today.

The foreman obviously takes the opportunity to ask everyone else in the team if they need more supplies. They do, and so he offers to get the supplies for the other tradesmen too.

Obviously, some insecure middle manager types, being obsessed with their own status, might see the 'boss' agreeing to run around to the suppliers as demeaning and want nothing to do with it.

However, the wily foreman knows that by doing so, he has kept the pace of the work (the velocity, as it is called in Scrum) going today, and, by buying the other supplies, has also removed other potential obstacles (called impediments in Scrum) for tomorrow's work. A side benefit is that the foreman also knows that he is only buying items for his project and not supplying items for someone else's project on the quiet (I told you he was wily). In other words, he has done some judicious budget management at the same time.

In Scrum leadership and management terms, the foreman's actions would be seen as a great success. The foreman (Scrum Master), has removed the immediate problems (impediments), kept the pace (velocity) of the work going, and has also removed potential problems (also impediments), for the other members of the team. Although he is unlikely to be aware of Scrum as a management framework, he has accidentally shown himself to be an excellent and effective Scrum Master.

On the other hand, the foreman _could_ have been so impressed by his own sense of importance that he would have said yes to the carpenter's request for them to go to the shops themselves, but this would have been at the expense of losing the momentum on the project.

Who really won? I think it was the foreman, how about you?

In reality, there are many times when every True Leader has to be a servant leader. It is amazing just how many of the very best leaders I have met and served have all said words to the effect of "it is an honour to serve you," to their staff. It doesn't mean they are a dogsbody; it means they serve them with their integrity, their knowledge and their wherewithal.

* * *

Rock n' Rollers as Servant Leaders?

On a completely different note, I once saw Bruce Springsteen and the E Street Band in a huge outdoor gig. You can't imagine a scenario that would be less of an example of a servant leader in action.

There were 40,000+ die-hard fans who had gone to see "The Boss," as even his fans call him. Just as they were coming to the end of the concert Bruce told his fans "it is always an honour to serve you." The crowd went wild.

I have no idea whether he was being genuine or not, although his long running reputation would suggest he was. If "The Boss" can be a servant leader, then so can I. How about you, Scrumnast?

Leadership - Extra Resources -

If we already know how to lead in a practical manner, why should you need any extra resources?

Well, sooner or later you are going to have to be interviewed to be another leader, or leaders, and these people probably couldn't lead a group of children into a sweet shop.

Nevertheless, they may well have heard of the following people below, so you should too. You are going to have to pass the interview so that's why I have included it here for you.

Here you go, good luck with getting that job.

W.C.H. Prentice

W.C.H. Prentice, a great leadership thinker, gave us this classic definition of what leadership is, all the way in 1961: *"The Accomplishment of a Goal through the direction of Human Assistants"*

I put his quote for two reasons:

1.   It's a great, concise, practical working definition of what leadership is. We can work with it and we can keep it in the back of our minds.

2. He was probably the very first person to say that leadership was more than just the result of possessing the physical power to be able to give someone a good kicking or being so much extraordinarily smarter than everybody else around.

W.C.H. Prentice's online article, **"Understanding Leadership,"** is tremendous. I urge you to go online and read it. You will learn more about leadership in its seven pages than by reading a bucket of other books on leadership. But it raises its own questions.

* * *

Like *how* do we actually direct the human assistants to accomplish the goal?

At this point, most books take some notes from some academics on what leadership is, but Leadership and Management are practical skills, not academic skills.

Instead, I think we are served better by some inspiring quotes from some truly great leaders who, being leaders, can actually tell us what they think leadership is.

I pepper the conversations I have with my teams with all of these. Perhaps you would like to as well

Here we go.

"Management is doing things right; leadership is doing the right thing." —*Peter F. Drucker*

"The supreme quality of leadership is integrity." —*Dwight D. Eisenhower*

"All of the great leaders have had one characteristic in common: it was the willingness to confront unequivocally the major anxiety of their people in their time. This, and not much else, is the essence of leadership." —*John Kenneth Galbraith*

"The task of leadership is not to put greatness into humanity, but to elicit it, for the greatness is already there." —*John Buchan (author of "The 39 Steps")*

"A leader is a person you will follow to a place you would not go by yourself." —*Joel Barker*

"A true leader has the confidence to stand alone, the courage to make tough decisions, and the compassion to listen to the needs of others. He does not set out to be a leader but becomes one by the equality of his actions and the integrity of his intent." —*Douglas MacArthur*

"A leader is best when people barely know he exists. When his work is done, his aim fulfilled, they will say: we did it ourselves." —*Lao Tzu*

* * *

"the aim of leadership should be to improve the performance of man and machine, to improve quality, to increase output, and simultaneously to bring pride of workmanship to people. Put in a negative way, the aim of leadership is not merely to find and record failures of men, but to remove the causes of failure: to help people to do a better job with less effort." — William Edwards Deming.

"The greatest leader is not necessarily the one who does the greatest things. He is the one that gets the people to do the greatest things." —Ronald Reagan

There you go, a bit more inspirational than asking an academic. I am not sure that anyone could add much more to define leadership than these quotations. Did you notice that quiet voice of humility that runs through all of them?

If we aspire to be anything like as good a leader as these were, humility is probably one of the qualities that we need to aspire to. Yet, when you consider the personalities of most leaders that you will actually encounter in business, it's not really humility that typically springs to mind, is it? So, who is right, the ex-leader giant of the free world, or today's chancer in a good suit?

I shall leave the last words to the American historian and classicist, Victor Davis Hansen. Being a Greek and Roman classicist, he's not an optimist on human nature, but he believes that good behaviour can shape your character.

For us leaders, I think that is an excellent aspiration.

"Deal in personal trust; your word is your bond; avoid extremes; treat the money you invest for others as something sacred; don't take any more perks than you would wish others to take; don't borrow what you couldn't suddenly pay back; imagine the worst case financial scenario and expect it may well happen; the wealthier you become the more humble you should act." - Victor Davis Hansen.

Leadership Extra Resources 2:

Daniel Goleman - Six Styles Of Leadership

I put this in here because a great many M.B.A. courses start off by talking about styles of leadership in their very first term and then set an essay on it so that the students can convince themselves that their, and their lecturer's, complete lack of personal charisma will not be a drawback[28] in being a leader.

Most leaders are not one particular style. They are an amalgam of the styles.

Being academics who couldn't run a whelk stall, the academics who set essays can't fathom that a leader can change their style as is needed, because that is *part of the job*. In fact, most leaders have very little trouble changing between them. Unlike academics…

The Visionary — mobilize people toward a vision. Works best when a clear direction or change is needed. The visionary promotes the most positive climate.

The Coaching — develop people for the future. Works best when helping people and building long-term strength. Again, promotes a positive climate.

The Affiliative — creates emotional bonds and harmony. Works best to heal rifts in teams or motivate people in stressful times. Also a positive climate.

The Democratic — builds consensus through participation. Works best to create consensus or get input. Also a positive climate.

The Pacesetting — expects excellence and self-direction. Works best to get quick results from a highly competent team. This type of leader promotes a negative climate.

---

[28] It will be. It really, really will be.

* * *

The Commanding — demand immediate compliance. Works best in crisis or with problematic people. Again a negative climate.

The most important aspect of these breakdowns is that since each style fits a different situation, a good leader needs to be able to switch between them when the context requires that. A leadership style becomes more of a tool, rather than just a personality trait.

There you go, you can now cite some references on leadership to people who don't know anything about leadership, but have the power to decide whether you know what you're talking about.

Best of luck - go get 'em!

FOCUS ON VALUE: TOMORROW'S MONEY - A STRATEGY

Time and the leader's responsibility.

Looking Near and Far At The Same Time: - Tomorrow's Money And How To Get There

If you have ever learned to drive, one of the hardest things to cope with is that you have to swap between looking at the next 20 feet in front of you and looking out about a quarter of a mile so that you can gauge what hazards are coming up.

It's really difficult skill to master. You convince yourself you will never be able to do it and then, one day, you just can.

Well, in a way a leader has to do the same thing with time: you have to look at what is happening today, concentrate on gathering in all the money but also keep an eye out for what you might expect to happen next month, next quarter, in six months, or a year away.

When we are consulting, we make business owners begin to understand this is we need them to think about *today*'s money and *tomorrow*'s money.

To use a different way of thinking about it, let's again think of our captain of the famous football team and what they have to do over time.

Before the game they must enthuse their players to give them belief that they can win

During every game he must also encourage them to do their best. And if they aren't winning, must inspire them to pick themselves up and redouble their efforts to try and win.

And after the game? They must celebrate with them, praising those that did exceptionally well and commiserating with those who didn't play well

* * *

Every successful captain must do these things during the game..

But that's not all they do, is it? There is a different dimension as well.

Think of what they do at the beginning of the season. Before any of the games are played they have to give their team mates belief that they have the heart and talent to win the championship.

As the season goes on they may have to adjust expectations until the end of the season where, hopefully they all lift the winnder's cup aloft.

In other words, there's the job during the game, and there's the job during the season and they are very different jobs because of the different time elements. In one they are focussed on the 90 minutes of the game and in the other they are focussed on the future.

And so it is in leadership.

There's a role for you in inspiring your team(s) during the work they are doing to get today's money in and there's a role in securing tomorrow's money too.

So how do we, as leaders focus on the future? What tools do we need?

We use the 80:20 analysis. Sometimes called the "Pareto analysis."

What is a Pareto Analysis?

It is a special kind of sales report, product report or any kind of business report.

An 80:20 report assumes that 20% of THESE things will be responsible for 80% of thoes things. Such as:
80% of your revenue will come from 20% of your customers.

80% of your revenue will come from 20% of your products

80% of your complaints will come from 20% of your customers

* * *

You get the idea.

I find that many of our clients, especially sales directors, hate 80:20 analysis. They like Top 10 reports. So why use it?

Well, here's a real life example. I once did an 80:20 analysis on a pharamceutical supplies company that made bandages etc. It had nearly 1,000 customers. However, when I did the analysis, we found that 80% of the sales went to 6 customers. When almost all your sales go to six customers, that isn't a business, that is a job.

Anyway, we will talk about that a little more over the page.

Tomorrow's Money

This is probably not for today. This is for tomorrow. There is a lot of work to get through before we get to tomorrow. But get there we will.

Getting a company or organisation to the stage where it is making enough money to sustain itself today is a remarkable thing. A rare thing.

If you and your team are making enough money to keep your heads above water? Fantastic. That is rare. I mean really rare. Sadly, most new limited companies fold within five years. And I am not just talking about small companies. Many large, even global companies can go bang too.

Getting to where you ares now has required a combination of great ideas, great marketing and messaging, great people making great products and services, great pricing and great managers and leaders.

Well done! - But for all your hard work, sweat and tears it is not enough to secure the future of you, your team and your company.

So where we are now is that your team is getting stuff done and you are getting paid for it, which means today's money is safe(-ish).

But what about tomorrow? Or next year? Or the year after that?

Here Be Dragons…

Part of your job as the leader is to shape thinking about where tomorrow's money is coming from. Why do we have to think about that?

Because nobody else is.

But surely, if we make money today then tomorow will take care of itself, right?

* * *

Wrong.

All the way back from Adam Smith writing his book on economics, "The Wealth of Nations," we have known that what makes up today's unique, boutique niche product or service will sooner or later be devalued and reduced in the market to the level of a commodity, like sugar, or petrol.

Why?

In a word, competition. Not just the competition you know about, but tomorrow's competition. And the day afterwards.

For every company that researches, develops brilliant new, unique products there are at least a hundred in your country that exist to steal your ideas and do them cheaper. And there are even more abroad.

In fact, that is why they are in business and it is how they do business.

Their business is copying great ideas and making "knock-offs." That is their business model and they are good at it. What's worse, they will probably make more money than you will while doing it. It is totally unfair and there's not much you can do about it.

That shiny new wonderful thing that changes the world and only you can make it? It is tomorrow's commodity.

Leaders need to be thinking about this because your practical people are busy being practical and earning your business today's money.

What can we do?

"Build It And They Will Come"

You could do the old "Build It And They Will Come" approach, as demonstrated in Kevin Costner's old film "Field Of Dreams." The basic idea is that you and a bunch of your people work in your spare time for months and months on a 'world beating' new product or service. Business journalists just love this story and this approach.

The problem with this approach is that ist is so dangerous.

Although it occasionally gives stratospheric results lots of businesses have gone bust doing it when the public were underwhelmed and didn't buy the products. Even Apple have used this approach in the early days and had some disasters with it. Let's be serious here, if Apple can't always make it work then it is unlikely that we can.

The "Willie Sutton" method:

When the twentieth century bank robber was asked why he robbed banks, Willie Sutton answered "Because that is where the money is."

And when it comes to guarding the future of your organisation that's a great strategy - go where the money is.

It's what we advise and help our clients with. I won't give away our trade secrets but this is what we do: We make them go up market and this is how we do it.

A strategy

1.   Find out who your very best customers are. Don't use a "Top 10 Best Customers" report - Go and do an 80:20 analysis on your customers. That can be frightening. I once did this for a client who had over 6,000 clients but it turned out that only 4 made up 80% of their business. That is scary. Concentrate ALL your next efforts on the clients who are making up that 80% of your income - forget the rest.

2.   Do what the very best marketers do, which is to take your very best customers and ask them why they like you and ask them else they'd love to buy from you.

* * *

3.   Go away and make some elastic band and sticking plaster type prototypes and ask your favourite clients what they think of them.

4.   If they like them then make a better prototype, again, refine it with your best clients. If they don't ask what they didn't like.

5.   If they like it then raise your prices - and stop offering discounts!

6.   Re do the 80:20 analysis every 13 weeks (it will probably take that long to see any changes, anyway) and do it four times a year.

In real life there's quite a bit more to it than that, but you get enough of an idea to begin to think seriously about doing it.

After all, tomorrow is coming.

SUMMARY

In Summary: The Leadernomics Crib Sheet:

Mobs:

A mob is a group of people without a leader. It is a short lived but dangerous thing. The behavoiur of a mob is always unpedictable and the group mood can turn on a hair. Mobs are hardly ever good - groups that have just lost ther leader can revert back teemporarily to a mob - You must try to avoid creating a mob at all costs

Mobs are so full of chaos and turmoil that those within them will look to each other for one or more leaders to emerge. The earliest part of that is when one or two "ringleaders" emerge. This does not tend to last very long but can be especially chaotic.

"Ringleaders" are the candidates who show up first as a mob starts to form and choose a leader. Most of them quickly fade into the background as one person is either chosen or the group acquiesces to someone's will.

Top tip: Groups of people abhor a leadership vaccuum. It is almost inevitable that leaders will emerge in a group because the mob are looking for one. You can ether accept this fact or get caught out by it.

British twentieth century management did not accept the fact that leaders are not the same as managers. They thought that management, sometimes called "Scientific Management," "Taylorism," or "Fordism," was enough to run large enterprises - they were foolhardy and very wrong, which is partly why we no longer have a home grown mass car industry in Britain.

What happened in the leadership vaccuum of the 1950s, 1960s, 1970s and the 1980s, is that the trade union shop stewards emerged as the leaders. If you Google videos of British industrial relations you will see how awful things can get when management and leadership are at loggerheads.

* * *

Leadership will happen so, because you now know how to be a great leader you need to be that person who is accepted by the group.

Which come First, Management or Leadership?

Remember, it is Leadership. Just look at our cousins the apes. Apes have leaders but aren't exactly known for being very good at agile management or bureaucracy. Leadership and managing small groups is natural for all of us primates and bureacracy is artificial, and unknown outside human beings.

Which is stronger, Leadership or management?

Leadership is stronger. Management can enforce or modify behaviours but leadership can bring forth (both great and monstrous) things from a group or population.

Followership:

People almost always act out of self interest - offer them (the people in the team) a better future than they think would otherwise enjoy and you won't have to push them - they will follow you.

Beware the "Theory X" attitude

Those 'leaders' who think that people only follow the money and that is all you have to get right are wrong. These people were once called "Theory X" managers. Project management is full of them. If you hear them mention the word 'resource,' you know you are in their company

Theory Y (MacGregor) and Sirota's "The Enthusiastic Employee"

They believe that people come to work for more than just money.

On top of the money they want:

1. Camaraderie - a sense of belonging
2. Achievement - they want their work to mean something
3. Equity   - they want no favoritism in their team

Get that right and they won't just follow you, they will stay with you when times are hard.

Please bear in mind that most ambitious people try to get ahead by making special friends with the boss. Do not fall for this, they are trying to manipulate you. By the way, everybody else in the team konws what they are doing - and they are watching (and judging) you.

Reluctant Leaders

As we have said in this book, I believe reluctant leaders to be the finest overlooked source of great leaders, especially if you are beginning to look at succession planning.

And if you were reluctant to put your first step on the ladder to becoming a leader then well done you. I have total respent for you.

And finally...

Before we say goodbye, will you indulge me for a minute? (There is a point, I promise).

This book, and my career, could not have been without Mr Marsh, a teacher I had when I was seven and a half years old.

He had been a soldier in the second world war. A very special soldier. He had started out as an infantry soldier but, it being a war he got promotion after promotion and ended up as an officer (captain) by the end of it. He was a very rare British man: he had risen though the ranks to become an officer. He had seen both sides of authority.

* * *

Because of what he saw and endured during the second world war, he thought leadership was a good thing to teach his kids and for them to learn.

When he had come back from the war, like many men of his generation, he dedicated the rest of his life to teaching, and to do his best to make sure that those he looked after would not make the same mistakes that his generation had.

We did not understand what he was talking about for most of the time. Mr Marsh was not a fan of what he called "peace time Officers." Being only seven, we didn't have a clue what he was talking about apart from it not being a good thing to be. However, being seven, and highly impessionable, the notion stuck with me down the decades.

On Friday afternoons, he would often go on and on about "peace time officers," and how they were an awful and terrible scourge to an Army, to a Navy and to an Air Force. Being seven, although we had no idea what a peace time officer was, - we knew it was not a good thing.

I understand what he meant now. What he meant by peace time officers are those people who are useless in themselves but brilliant at playing office politics and getting themselves promoted far higher than their competence would allow.

In the 1970s, there was common talk of Laurencce J. Peter's 1969 book, "The Peter Principle," which which states that managers are promoted two levels above their actual level of competence or until they reach the "Peter Plateau." I think it's definitely worth a read.

This is a problem in Britain today. We have a plague of useless managers. And I do not just mean middel managers. We have no end of useless, incompetent, dead legs in positions of power. They like to call themselves 'the elite,' but they are not the elite. They are merely the true 'useless eaters' in our society.

But that's okay. You know why? You and I are the descendants of giants. Your great, great, great, great grandparents did great things. They built institutions like hospital Saturday funds, insurance companies, mortgage companies and libraries of books that that the government took over.

They built canals, bridges, railway engines, railways, roads, lorries and cars. Men in boiler suits. Not BMW and Audi drivers in suits

Just like your ancestors did, we can do this again. We really can build back better. It's just that we have to do it for ourselves. But that's okay, isn't it? We always knew in our hearts it would be like that.

My grandfather used to say to me "the reason that we have the leaders we have is that most of the people who could be great leaders don't want to lead."

Being eight or nine at the time, I didn't know what he was talking about but it obviously stayed with me and decades later, I now know what he meant. But why do those who could be great leaders not want to lead?

Is it that they don't want the responsibility? No, I don't think so. I think the reason is that like the vast majority of people, they hold leadership in contempt because of the example set by most leaders. They don't want to be seen in the same light as them and, while they are about it, frankly, they'd also really rather not ruin other peoples' lives, either.

Well, that luxury has passed us by. Now we need to stand up and lead. But leadership is not so hard, is it? Look at the picture over the page...

See what I mean?

* * *

"Milk Monitors" from the late 1960s

If these little guys can take responsibility to get their things done then you and I have no excuse, do we?

Take care

Nick Hewyn Holmes - January 2025

X: @HewynNick
Substack: substack.com/@nickhewynholmes
Rumble: Hewyn
Youtube: Hewyn1
Web:
www.nickhewynholmes.com
www.scrumnastics.co.uk